ILLUSTRATED HISTORY OF THE

BANTAM BOOKS

TORONTO • NEW YORK • LONDON • SYDNEY • AUCKLAND

RIVERINE FORCE

by
John Forbes and Robert Williams

GIANT SLINGSHOT

A water cannon fires into an enemy bunker on the Vam Co Dong River during Operation Giant Slingshot. The water cannon was one of the more unusual weapons that proved perfect for riverine use. It was used with considerable ingenuity to dislodge the enemy from well-built earth and log bunkers, which were usually immune to all but flamethrowers and the heaviest artillery.

ROCKET ATTACK

The view from the cockpit of a UH 1-B as its rockets home in on suspected enemy targets on the banks of the Bassac River in the Mekong Delta. Close air support by helicopter was a vital element in the success of the Mobile Riverine Force. Helicopters prevented patrol boats from blundering into ambushes and provided covering fire when they did.

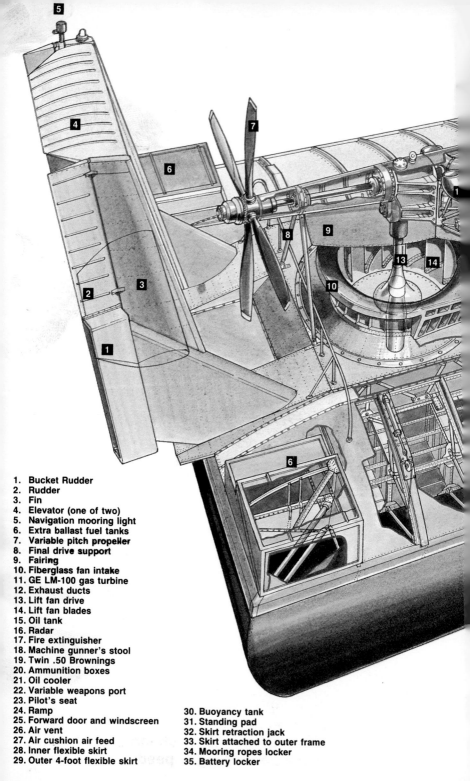

1. Bucket Rudder
2. Rudder
3. Fin
4. Elevator (one of two)
5. Navigation mooring light
6. Extra ballast fuel tanks
7. Variable pitch propeller
8. Final drive support
9. Fairing
10. Fiberglass fan intake
11. GE LM-100 gas turbine
12. Exhaust ducts
13. Lift fan drive
14. Lift fan blades
15. Oil tank
16. Radar
17. Fire extinguisher
18. Machine gunner's stool
19. Twin .50 Brownings
20. Ammunition boxes
21. Oil cooler
22. Variable weapons port
23. Pilot's seat
24. Ramp
25. Forward door and windscreen
26. Air vent
27. Air cushion air feed
28. Inner flexible skirt
29. Outer 4-foot flexible skirt
30. Buoyancy tank
31. Standing pad
32. Skirt retraction jack
33. Skirt attached to outer frame
34. Mooring ropes locker
35. Battery locker

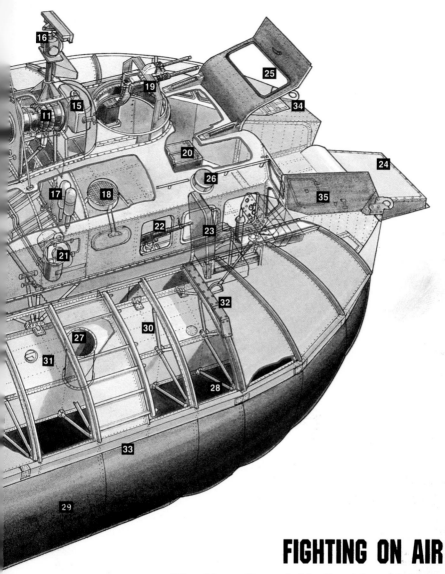

FIGHTING ON AIR

The Navy Patrol Air Cushion Vehicle (PACV), or Hovercraft, was the technically most advanced vehicle used in riverine warfare. Part boat, part helicopter, and part airplane, the then experimental Bell PACV could skim on rubber skirts over the water on a 4-foot-thick bubble of air at 60 knots. The three craft used on combat trials proved perfect for amphibious warfare, and led to much larger craft being developed for high-speed beach assault.

BIG ZIPPO

An orange ribbon of napalm belches into an evening sky as an Assault Support Patrol Boat (ASPB) fires its flamethrower. Fitted on monitors and ASPBs, flamethrowers proved indispensable in riverine warfare. They were especially effective in the confined spaces of otherwise impregnable enemy bunkers with the flame jet rapidly burning up all the available oxygen.

INTO THE RUNG SAT

US Marines in outboard motor boats prepare to enter the Rung Sat, an ancient pirate haven known as "The Forest of the Assassins," during a 1,200-man search-and-clear operation in 1966. Designated a Special Zone, the Rung Sat's tangled maze of tiny inlets and mangrove swamps provided the enemy with a staging post on the strategically vital route between Saigon and the sea.

EDITORS: Richard Grant, Richard Ballantine. PHOTO RESEARCH: John Moore.
DRAWINGS: John Batchelor. MAPS: Peter Williams. STUDIO: Kim Williams.
PRODUCED BY: The Up & Coming Publishing Company, Bearsville, New York.

RIVERINE FORCE
THE ILLUSTRATED HISTORY OF THE VIETNAM WAR
A Bantam Book/ December 1987

ACKNOWLEDGEMENTS
*The authors wish to thank Edward J. Marolda and G. Wesley Pryce III of
the Naval Historical Center in Washington, D.C., for their help, good
advice, and assistance in securing hitherto unpublished documents; also the
Center for Military History in Washington provided invaluable assistance and
access to many hours of after-combat tapes.*

*The photographs for this book were selected from the archives of DAVA,
USMC, and the personal collection of
Colonel Victor J. Croizat, USMC (Ret).*

Library of Congress Cataloging-in-Publication Data

Forbes, John, 1954–
    Riverine force : [illustrated history of the Vietnam War] / by
John Forbes and Robert Williams.
    p.   cm.
    ISBN 0-553-34317-3
    1. Vietnamese Conflict, 1961–1975—Riverine operations, American .
2. United States. Navy—History—Vietnamese Conflict, 1961–1975.
I. Williams, Robert.   II. Title.
DS558.7.F67   1987
959.704'33'73—dc19   87-27649
                                                                CIP

Published simultaneously in the United States and Canada

*Bantam Books are published by Bantam Books, Inc. Its trademark, consisting of the
words "Bantam Books" and the portrayal of a rooster, is Registered in U.S. Patent
and Trademark Office and in other countries. Marca Registrada. Bantam Books, Inc.,
666 Fifth Avenue, New York, New York 10103.*

PRINTED IN THE UNITED STATES OF AMERICA

CW   0   9   8   7   6   5   4   3   2   1

Contents

The first shots

THE DELTA of the Mekong River can be likened to a man's hand with twisted fingers; the fingers are the four main streams that run into the South China Sea while the Ca Mau peninsula, projecting to the south, looks on a map like an enormous swollen thumb.

It is a unique environment, laced with millions of streams, canals, and cuts, each lined with trees, usually mangrove or nipa palm. From the air this vast flat expanse looks wide open; but at water level it seems often cramped and claustrophobic.

Its people live on the water; in some densely inhabited areas the land is always underwater. From the air these areas look like flood disaster zones: The houses are built on stilts; even the rice crops float on extended roots.

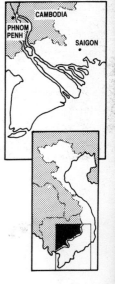

The river is always changing. Shoals and sandbars shift, appear, and disappear. The water's color and smell changes with the season. At times great rafts of pink, white, and red hibiscus flowers fill the air with perfume. Even the view can change dramatically with the water level. The only constant is the steaming heat.

By the 1960s, helped by a drainage and resettlement program carried out in the last years of French colonial rule, the Mekong Delta had become the heartland and rice barrel of South Vietnam. At the end of the decade its population numbered nine million: more than one-half of the whole country's. The people literally lived on mud: silt and soil washed from the river banks in China, Burma, Thailand, Laos, and Cambodia in the Mekong's 2,600-mile journey from the eastern Himalayas to the South China Sea. The mud was often 200 feet thick, and it made the Delta one of the most fertile and

strategically valuable food-producing areas in Asia, serviced by one of the densest networks of inland waterways in the world.

More than 80 percent of South Vietnam's rice crop was harvested in the Delta, and when the US first became militarily involved in the region much of the rice was going straight to the Viet Cong Communist guerrillas. In 1964 South Vietnam was one of the world's major rice exporters; by 1967 it imported almost a million tons; up to twice that amount was being diverted for consumption by the Communists.

It was in this remarkable and unique environment

The first shots

NARROW WATERS:
A US Navy river patrol boat team heads into a typical Mekong Delta canal. Note the way the second boat is waiting at the entrance to the canal, to reduce the danger of both boats getting trapped by an ambush. Canalside trees have been stripped by defoliant.

that the US Navy was called to fight a campaign with weapons strange to a force used to spanning the oceans with battleships and aircraft carriers. The brown-water war in South Vietnam was a small-unit war fought in mud and creek and canal with patrol boats and an odd assortment of almost reptile-like armored craft.

The story of the Navy's riverine campaign is the story of a journey into the Delta, a bloody voyage from the coastal waters, then into the mouths of the big rivers, beginning to probe the narrower streams, and finally pushing far upstream, past islands and

The first shots

THE DELTA:
One of the great waterways of Southeast Asia, the Mekong begins life in the snowmelt of the Tibetan plateau before making its 2,500-mile journey to the sea through China, Laos, Cambodia, and South Vietnam where it divides into four rivers. Although the Mekong travels barely 160 miles through South Vietnam, its waters feed a vast life-supporting network of canals, many less than 6 feet deep at low water.

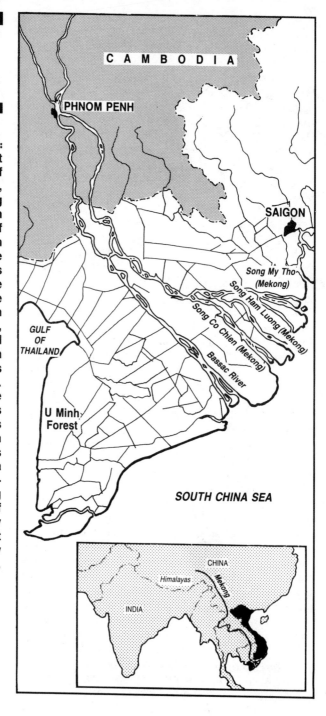

C A M B O D I A

PHNOM PENH

SAIGON

Song My Tho (Mekong)

Song Ham Luong (Mekong)

Song Co Chien (Mekong)

Bassac River

GULF OF THAILAND

U Minh Forest

SOUTH CHINA SEA

CHINA

Himalayas

Mekong

INDIA

fishing villages, jungle and swamp, through the heart of enemy territory, and to the heart of the war.

The first to realize the possibilities offered by riverine operations in Indochina were the French during their nine-year struggle to maintain colonial rule over Vietnam after World War II. They were finally forced out of Vietnam by their morale-shattering strategic defeat at Dien Bien Phu in May 1954. But behind them the French left an understanding of the tactics they had successfully evolved in their battles with the Viet Minh Communists in the Red River Delta of North Vietnam. These tactics recognized waterways as the roads of Vietnam, lines of communication to be utilized rather than obstacles to be crossed.

The French used the waterways to give mobility both to troops and heavy weapons, which had become increasingly vulnerable to mines and ambush on the roads. Formations of wheeled and tracked land combat vehicles were replaced on the water by "dinassauts" (naval assault divisions). These units generally included a ship, such as a large landing ship, for command and fire support; six or more armored landing craft modified from World War II equipment, some as troop-carriers, some—called "monitors"— with particularly heavy armor and weapons; and at least one FOM light patrol boat or river minesweeper. These dinassauts were the nucleus of the brown-water navy inherited by the new government of South Vietnam under premier Ngo Dinh Diem when he came to power in 1954 after the departure of the French.

The US Navy was to follow in the wake of the French, and then extend their techniques. At first the Americans operated an offshore blockade, and merely supplied advisors to the Vietnamese forces struggling for survival on the inland waterways. They were quickly drawn inland, into mobile operations on the French pattern, and finally were able to use the rivers in a way that the French had never managed, and to create patrolled lines all around the Delta, which effectively became barriers that the Communists crossed at their peril.

Elsewhere in South Vietnam riverine forces were used to provide valuable support for ground forces, particularly in operating secure supply lines on waterways when roads became too dangerous. The

Jungle stream —French colonial troops fording a stream in the Red River Delta of North Vietnam in 1953. The French quickly learned that it made more tactical sense to travel along rivers than to try to cross them.

FOREST DEPTHS: A French "FOM" light patrol boat tunnels through overhanging creepers and foliage to push along a Delta stream. Americans used large quantities of defoliants to clear the banks of cover for ambushes. At the time Navy men welcomed the feeling of security a wide-open bank provided.

Americans took up the burden of training, equipping, and advising the South Vietnamese armed forces in the continuing struggle against the Communists in 1956, two years after the fall of Dien Bien Phu.

Following a US development plan the Vietnamese Navy reinforced its river force to six dinassauts, now renamed River Assault Groups (RAGs) and also set up an offshore patrol designed to cut the flow of northern arms and supplies to the guerrillas, now known as Viet Cong (VC or Victor Charlie in the phonetic alphabet, later simply Charlie).

By 1960 it had become apparent that the political existence of an independent South Vietnam was seriously threatened by the Communists, and the advisory effort was stepped up. The advisors were authorized to serve in the field, and in 1961 so were up to 8,000 American support troops and three companies of helicopters. The advisors were not only there to improve the performance of the Vietnamese units: They acted as liaison officers to help co-operation with American units. And it was the advisors' reports on the low effectiveness of the South Vietnamese military that finally convinced the Pentagon that there was no alternative but to step up direct US involvement in what was to become a damaging and drawn-out conflict.

Extracts from the log of one advisor, serving with the Vietnamese Navy's coastal forces patrolling the coastline to intercept VC supplies being moved by sea, give an impression of incompetence bordering on corruption, of a unit more intent on avoiding the enemy than hindering it.

> 9 September: Delivered pastries to HQ 401. Commanding Officer ran ship aground. Able to get off. . .
> 19 September: We had been following a track laid out by the CO (commanding officer) on course roughly perpendicular to the coast. . . I asked the CO if he expected to find junk traffic on this track. He replied: "No, I'm just cruising."

Another advisor reported that his patrol speed was just four knots, ostensibly because of the danger of night navigation without radar. "Daytime patrol speed also 4 kt because, according to the South Vietnamese CO, "it is not necessary to go faster." It is

POOR RELATION: A Vietnamese Navy Sea Force PGM motor gunboat heads for the sea from base at Kim Quy. The Sea Force was created as a result of pressure from the French, not because the Vietnamese felt any need to have a blue-water navy, and as a result was never given adequate men or resources by the Saigon government.

'too dangerous' to darken ship. Also 'VC won't be suspicious if we have lights showing.' "

The coastal forces had particular problems, chiefly because they were a purely navy command, and the Vietnamese Navy was a long way last in the pecking order for promotion, status, and resources—making it the least attractive service for any ambitious and capable young officer hoping to work his way up the Saigon military establishment. By contrast, the river forces were under Army control, which had a greater call on South Vietnam's resources.

The advisors operating on the inland rivers with the RAGs had a different story to tell, one often of dedication and courage among Vietnamese sailors with long experience in riverine combat. These men would respond readily to the leadership qualities that some of the young Americans brought to their training task.

One of the outstanding American characters of those early days was Lieutenant Harold Dale Meyerkord, who inspired the men of RAG 23 with his extraordinary heroism. He was posthumously awarded the Navy Cross, but the medal was not won by a single act of courage in the middle of battle but by the qualities he revealed in the few short months of his demanding duties.

His personal combat log for 13 August 1964, his first firefight, shows the coolness that characterized his approach to action.

TEAM TALK: A US Navy lieutenant advisor and his Vietnamese counterpart plan an amphibious raid on a Viet Cong unit off the Co Chien River with Vietnamese Navy Coastal Group junk units. The junk sailors, a paramilitary militia force until 1964, would carry out land operations themselves, after beaching their craft, and their advisors went with them.

0600 Arrive at Bassac ferry and embark 60 Civil Guard troops. . . 270 Company Vinh Long Civil Guard. . .

0900 Under way up Mang Thit river for Tam Binh. Battle preparations are made. All guns manned and loaded. Dai Huy (Lieutenant Commander) Nguyen Van Hoa puts on his helmet and flak vest. The river is very narrow and because our command post is on the open deck of the monitor we are vulnerable to small arms fire. I don't wear a helmet or flak vest. My preparation consists of setting my carbine on auto and loading it with a clip of tracers. These I will use to direct fire. Boats are now in formation. First, 100 yards in front are the two FOM light patrol boats, then the Monitor, then at 50 yard intervals are the two troop-carriers and last is the LCM heavy landing craft. All boats now fly the Jolly Roger. The river RATS (assault troops) love to fly a skull and cross bones in combat. . .

1120 Viet Cong opened fire on 2 FOMs. Fire from Vinh Binh side. As the Monitor moved up to support the FOMs the transports landed their troops south of the ambush. The FOMs ran into the shore at the ambush point, sweeping the area with .30 cal and .50 cal machine gun fire. The Monitor began firing into the ambush with 40mm and .50 cal machine guns. The 40mm was directed by me with a carbine firing tracers. The troops hit the VC from the south. The VC withdrew into a cane brake. . .

1200 Lost contact. Boats and troops continued north. . ."

A US advisor to Junk Division 33 eating his meal in the officers' mess near Ly Nhon. He is wearing black pajamas, the classic garb of Vietnamese peasant and sailor—and Viet Cong guerrilla. Vietnamese food was an acquired taste, usually rice smothered in "nuoc mom," a strong fish sauce.

Many times in the course of his 30 firefights Meyerkord turned defeat into victory by the power of his example.

On 30 November 1964, he discovered a VC canal block in the course of a reconnaissance under fire, and immediately set up an improvised command post on shore. He coordinated artillery fire and air strikes, blasting a path through the ambush, then organized medical evacuation helicopters to care for the casualties—relatively few in number, thanks to his initiative and quick thinking.

On 13 January 1965, he took to a small boat in

the middle of a firefight, leaving his command craft to administer first aid to the wounded on a boat that had run aground in Viet Cong territory. Ten days later he took control of a River Force flotilla when the commander was hit in an ambush, and although wounded himself ran the operation for an hour until victory was assured. In his last action, typically, he had placed himself in the lead boat of a column to set an example for the Vietnamese personnel. He was wounded by the first shots of the inevitable ambush, but continued to exchange fire with the enemy at point-blank range until he was again wounded, this time mortally.

The first shots

WATCHFUL EYE: Lieutenant Harold Dale Meyerkord (right) looks on as a diver of his River Assault Group 23 prepares to enter the water during salvage operations. The stern of a monitor and a light landing craft can be seen in the background. Lieutenant Meyerkord was killed two months after this picture was taken, posthumously winning the Navy Cross.

Despite the advisors' experiences with the Vietnamese riverine forces, and perhaps underestimating the potential importance of the river war in Vietnam, the US Navy in the mid-1960s was ill-prepared for small-scale small-boat operations in brown waters. But once these operations started, it took just three years—from the spring of 1965 to the fall of 1968—for the Navy to penetrate the furthest reaches of the narrow twisted waterways of South Vietnam. The deployment was a hurried affair, involving much improvisation of equipment, organization, and tactics, but the result was one of the tactical and strategic success stories of the Vietnam War.

Closing the sea lanes

THE NAVY was in at the very start of the large-scale US involvement in southeast Asia that in the Gulf of Tonkin incident, when raiding North Vietnamese torpedo boats attacked the destroyer USS *Maddox*. The background of the attack remains disputed, but as far as the US Congress was concerned it was the last straw in a series of provocative acts by the North Vietnamese, and the result, on 7 August 1964, was a joint resolution by both houses of Congress, authorizing the president to use all measures, including armed force, to assist the defense of South Vietnam.

The Gulf of Tonkin resolution became the constitutional key that would allow President Johnson and later President Nixon a free hand to run the war as they saw fit. The Navy had already begun to look seriously at what its role in the theater was going to be. In January 1964 Captain Phillip H. Bucklew, USN, was sent to Saigon at the head of an eight-man study team. His report stated that the Vietnamese coastal patrols were failing to stop the Communists shipping in men and munitions by sea, and would have to be augmented by the US Navy; it noted the need for a blockade on inland waterways to cut the supply routes from Cambodia to Vietnam; and it suggested that US forces might be needed to help patrol other inland waterways.

His conclusions were prophetic, and to a great extent provided a blueprint for future Navy conduct of the war.

At this time the US Navy's operational involvement in Vietnam was extremely limited. Approximately 150 advisors reporting to the Naval Advisory Group (NAG) in Saigon were serving with all the different elements of the Vietnamese Navy,

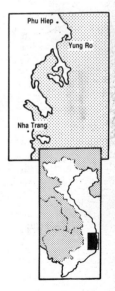

Closing the sea lanes

INTERCEPTED:
Landing craft cluster around a captured North Vietnamese trawler to unload ammunition and supplies destined for the Viet Cong. Earlier US patrol boats had forced the trawler to run aground off the Mekong Delta. Its crew had unsuccessfully tried to set the trawler on fire to prevent its cargo being captured.

and approximately 100 more men were involved in Special Forces training and SEABEE Technical Assistance Teams on civic works projects. Pacific fleet support for the Vietnamese Navy's offshore patrols had been withdrawn in 1962 because seaborne infiltration by the Viet Cong of men and supplies was thought to be insignificant.

The advisors did not have command over Vietnamese forces at a local level, although in Saigon the Vietnamese high command knew that it had to

heed the advice of the American headquarters in Vietnam, the Military Assistance Command Vietnam (MACV). The result was an unwieldy structure that often left American personnel in the position of spectators, helpless to prevent the blunders of others. If they wanted to influence the course of operations it was frequently only possible by contacting Saigon.

Where coastal operations were concerned the situation was made even more complex by the fact

Gen. William C. Westmoreland —on board the helicopter landing ship USS *Princeton* in late 1964 during flood relief operations. The US commander in Vietnam, Westmoreland took a strong interest in the Navy's Vietnam strategy as intelligence reports increasingly demonstrated the importance of maritime supply lines to the Viet Cong.

that the Vietnamese Navy had two different commands involved: the Sea Force and a former junk militia, the Coastal Force. US responsibilities were also split between the Saigon-based Military Assistance Command Vietnam, which concerned itself directly with operational matters; the Naval Advisory Group, which administered the advisory program; and the Pacific Fleet, whose commander in chief was based in Honolulu.

The whole setup was far from satisfactory, as Captain Bucklew had discovered, but it took a specific incident to establish the need for the US Navy to become involved in coastal operations.

On 16 February 1965, the pilot of a US Army medevac helicopter spotted a suspicious-looking ship in Vung Ro Bay, near Nha Trang, some 300 miles south of the demilitarized zone (DMZ) that divided North from South Vietnam. The Vietnamese had their coastline divided into defensive zones, so the pilot informed the senior US advisor at Coastal Defense Zone 2 headquarters in Nha Trang, Lieutenant Commander Harvey P. Rodgers, of the sighting. Following the cumbersome procedures then in force, Rodgers told his Vietnamese colleagues, and they then asked the Vietnamese Air Force to confirm the report. Eventually three air strikes left the ship aground. A fourth was called on a nearby beach after ground fire was reported coming from it.

The Vietnamese coastal zone commander then arranged for an Army detachment to be carried by sea to investigate the situation the following day.

Air strikes and illumination were requested for the night, to try to hinder any Viet Cong attempts to unload the stranded trawler. These were not provided, and lights and activity were reported in the area. The next morning the failures on the part of the Vietnamese continued. A detachment of the Army was detailed to travel to the bay by sea, but the commander refused to embark his men because he thought the Vung Ro area was too strongly held by the Viet Cong. The ship sailed without troops, and found it impossible to enter the bay because of heavy fire. The following day a conference was held attended by US high command representatives, and a more businesslike plan evolved, using two battalions of the South Vietnamese Army (ARVN) to attack overland, while a Special Forces company, already in the area, landed near the grounded ship.

Meanwhile the grounded ship was destroyed by gunfire from the Special Forces landing ship and a patrol boat that had been ordered to the scene. The following day the landing ship was twice beaten off by heavy fire, but finally got into a beach near the wrecked trawler to land the Special Forces company. A large cache of weapons was found on shore, but, despite protests by US advisors, all troops withdrew as night fell. The ARVN remained in the area for another five days, and despite the several opportunities the Viet Cong were given to dispose of material stored in the area, some 100 tons of ammunition and medical supplies were found on the wreck of the ship and in nearby dumps.

The quantities suggested that more than one shipload was involved. Further investigation showed that similar weapons to those found at Vung Ro were turning up in locations widely scattered along the coast, indicating that material was being landed at more than one place.

All this new evidence helped remove any lingering illusions the Pentagon had about the efficiency of the Vietnamese Navy's coastal patrols at stopping Viet Cong smuggling.

What is more, the quantities of equipment involved were enough to send a shiver down the spine of the MACV. General Westmoreland, MACV commander, called the commander-in-chief Pacific and his Navy commander to a crisis meeting ten days after the Vung Ro incident to discuss exactly how the US Navy proposed to cut the enemy supply lines.

The conference split the problem in two: first, the inshore infiltration of VC craft among the 50,000 civilian boats operating in Vietnamese coastal waters; second, the big steel-hulled trawlers of the type caught at Vung Ro. The first aspect, it was decided somewhat optimistically, could continue to be handled by the Vietnamese Navy, with some assistance. The second was clearly a task for US Navy ships and aircraft.

As a result of that conference, in just four months the basic structure of naval operations in Vietnam would be complete. The US Joint Chiefs of Staff approved these findings on 16 March, and the same day two destroyers took up station for patrol duty

Nerve center —Maps and radio equipment dominate the coastal surveillance center at Vung Tau, just north of the Mekong Delta. One of six surveillance centers, it was in constant contact with American and Vietnamese ships and aircraft. It was up to them to ensure that any suspect vessels sighted were not allowed to escape inspection.

Closing the sea lanes

THE BIG SEARCH: South Vietnamese junk force men, one carrying a Thompson sub-machine gun, start to search a fishing boat for arms, while another sampan waits its turn. INSET: Notice displayed by a nervous junk captain hoping to save his boat from damage.

off the northern and southern borders of Vietnam. Simultaneously, Navy patrol planes deployed to Ton Son Nhut air base outside Saigon, and began to fly surveillance patrols to guide and supplement the destroyers' efforts. The operation, run by the Pacific Fleet, was code named Market Place as of March 24, 1965.

Within a month there were 28 ships in the Vietnam Patrol Force, Task Force 71, on the blockade. The unit existed just three months before it was

WE ARE IN A VERY FRAGILE BOAT
DO NOT APPROACH US WITH YOUR SHIP
SEND YOUR LIGHT BOAT AND COME
TO CHECK US IF YOU PLEASE
THANK YOU VERY MUCH

Junk base —The Vietnamese Navy Coastal Force junks were divided into divisions of around 20 boats, operating out of bases like this one at Co Luy. At sea the junkmen faced frequent storms in craft less than 50 feet long, and their land bases were regularly attacked. The result was crippling desertion rates that meant that fewer than half the 500-plus vessels in the force were ever at sea.

superseded by the Vietnam-based Task Force 115. The Navy established five Coastal Surveillance Centers; the northernmost at Da Nang, while to the south were bases at Qui Nhon, Nha Trang, and Vung Tau and one at An Thoi on Phu Quoc island off the Cambodian border.

In the early days these centers spent much of their time coordinating the operations of the Seventh Fleet elements off the coast with the US Naval Advisory Group and the Vietnamese Navy HQ in Saigon, the principal sources of intelligence. It was an unsatisfactory command structure that was not to last. The question of the inshore patrol soon reared its head again, for it was still obvious that the Vietnamese Navy at its current state of equipment and training was not capable of providing remotely watertight blockades. The Seventh Fleet lacked both the manpower and the specialized small craft needed for such an operation, and the next proposal was that the US Coast Guard should come to the rescue. On 29 April 1965, seventeen 82-foot Coast Guard cutters, designated WPBs were ordered to Vietnam.

At the same time it was finally decided, to order some specialized patrol boats that would take the US Navy into the brown waters of the rivers of Vietnam.

The first ground combat unit to fight in Vietnam under the Stars and Stripes, the 9th Marine Expeditionary Brigade, had landed at Da Nang just over one month before, on 8 March. In July the final essential step was taken, and the blockade's headquarters was moved "in country," under command of the chief, Naval Advisory Group, MACV, and renamed Market Time, Task Force 115.

When the US Navy took on the Market Time patrol the Viet Cong were largely supplied by sea. This was not so much the result of the vigilance of the South Vietnamese Army as of the poor state of the road network in Indochina. In Vietnam's underdeveloped economy the waterborne sampans were as vital as trucks in moving freight in a country where the bulk of the population lived in the deltas of the Mekong River and the Red River, with their elaborate canal networks.

When Admiral Norvell G. Ward took command of Task Force 115 on 31 July 1965, the enemy had 25 steel-hulled trawlers in its Naval Transportation Group 115, each trawler shipping two 100-ton

cargoes of weapons and ammunition a month into VC-held areas like the Ca Mau peninsula in the deep south. This system was satisfying an estimated 70 percent of the guerrillas' needs.

At first the Market Time forces were barely sufficient to stop the flow. When Admiral Ward took over they consisted of just seven radar picket ships, two minesweepers, three LSTs (converted tank landing ships) providing radar cover off the mouths of the Mekong, and seventeen of the newly arrived WPB Coast Guard cutters. This force could not have managed without the support of five P-2 Neptune patrol aircraft flying from Tan Son Nhut, a few P-5M Marlin seaplanes, and P-3 Orions, based at Langley Point in the Philippines. The planes patrolled far out to sea, where they could provide early warning of the big trawlers, while the ships were deployed in nine areas running 30 to 40 miles out from the coast and

OCEAN GOING: The deep-water minesweeper USS *Pledge.* An awning has been rigged over the rear deck to protect the inspection team from the sun, and plenty of rubber tires are on the side to cushion the ship from the junks and sampans that come alongside.

RUNNING FOR COVER: A seemingly harmless North Vietnamese fishing trawler; at right, the same ship destroyed after trying to escape the Coast Guard cutter. About 250 tons of arms and ammunition were on board.

an average of 100 miles along it. The bulk of the patrols were concentrated in two zones: off the Cambodian border in the Gulf of Thailand, and off the DMZ north of Da Nang. Here the small number of WPBs available were used to stop and search every boat that might be carrying supplies or personnel to aid the Viet Cong. These were the "barrier" patrols, providing nonstop 24-hour surveillance with boats, ships, and planes over the key sectors for VC smuggling operations.

The WPBs worked out of An Thoi in the south and Da Nang in the north. Along the 1,000 miles of coastline between these two points, the only US Navy presence was the big destroyers and ocean minesweepers, but they were limited to operating

in deep water well offshore. Inshore patrols were mounted by approximately 200 motor junks and a handful of Vietnamese Navy Sea Force patrol boats. Even with American advisors these forces were not providing adequate cover.

It was becoming clear that the US Navy eventually would have to run patrols closer inshore, and into the larger rivers and waterways—strategic communications channels that were increasingly regarded as Communist territory, along with most of the Mekong Delta.

This would be a job for the PCF Swift fast patrol boats, none of which were yet in Vietnam. These were to be the first specialized patrol craft used by the US Navy in the theater, based on the design of

GOFERS:
One of the 17 US Coast Guard cutters sent to South Vietnamese in 1965. Overpainted in war zone gray instead of their customary white, they were the first boats to be used on the barrier patrols off the DMZ and the Cambodian border. Their outstanding characteristic was seaworthiness, which meant they went wherever the weather was worst.

a commercial oil-rig service launch hurriedly adapted for naval use.

The PCFs were a success even before they arrived in country. A purely mathematical study had proved that the 20 boats ordered in the spring of 1965 would be hopelessly inadequate and the order was raised first to 54 boats, and then to 84, before even one of them had arrived.

This last increase was a result of a conference of senior Navy officers held in Saigon in September 1965. At that meeting it was concluded that the military situation in South Vietnam warranted an increase in the Navy effort. Recommendations were made to increase the number of offshore patrol ships from 9 to 14, to double the number of patrol aircraft, and to call up another 9 WPBs. It was also proposed to add another LST to the three keeping radar watch on the mouths of the Mekong to ensure continuous coverage of these critical gateways to the Delta.

Finally, and most radically, the conference recommended that a 120-boat river patrol force be established, based on LSTs anchored off the Mekong, with a mission to patrol up to 25 miles inland. This force, whose creation was approved in December 1965, was to become the Game Warden task force—manned by sailors in olive green army-style fatigues and the black berets that were to provide their

nickname. By the end of 1965 a comprehensive organization for coastal surveillance had been put into operation, and the inshore patrols were being strengthened daily as new PCF units completed their training and came into service. Furthermore, the US Navy had continued its effort to improve the standards of training and equipment of the Vietnamese Navy. The number of advisors had grown to the point where every Sea Force ship sailed with an American on board, with more than 90 advisors serving with the 28 junk units of the Coastal Force. The Vietnamese Navy was still of mixed quality, but in the long term this was an investment of resources that had to pay off if the US was ever to hand the war over to its ally.

Aerial search —A P-2 Orion circles above a couple of junks, ready to radio back its position to one of the coastal surveillance centers.

The increased size of the Market Time operation and the growing complexity of the Navy's contribution to the war meant that the Naval Advisory Group in Saigon no longer had the resources to provide a suitable command structure, and on 1 April 1966, a new command, US Naval Forces Vietnam (NavForV) came into being, headed by Rear Admiral Alfred G. Ward. Market Time, Task Force 115, was handed over to Captain Clifford L. Stewart, USN.

During this period the patrol barrier was further refined, with the area divided into three zones: an air surveillance sector farthest out to sea, which was augmented by island-based radar stations; the outer surface barrier patrolled by large ships; and inshore a mixture of PCFs, WPBs, and Vietnamese Navy boats and junks. The bigger ships on the outer barrier with their superior radar and navigational equipment were expected to help and direct the lighter boats, reinforcing them if necessary with their heavier firepower.

Simultaneously the protection of harbors by boat patrols and undersea surveillance was brought into Market Time under the code name Operation Stable Door.

Within the first few months of Market Time the WPBs saw combat. Ship-to-ship firefights were not uncommon as the big trawlers tried to outrun the blockade ships. But in a very short space of time the North Vietnamese realized that the party was over as far as large-scale seaborne supply was concerned, and the routine for many patrol boat crews became one of boredom and discomfort. Swift boats

would usually patrol 24 to 30 hours between crew changes. By exchanging crews and refuelling from support ships a Swift could stay at sea for ten days or more. For the minesweepers and radar pickets, and the bigger high-endurance cutters when they came into service, the periods could be much longer. Once on station the boat or ship had little to do but cover its sector at a steady cruise, keeping a visual and radar lookout, and approach every boat or ship sighted, occasionally ordering a junk alongside or

Closing the sea lanes

THE SWIFTS: Recently arrived PCFs in formation in the Gulf of Thailand. Capable of 25 knots, they were based on a commercially available hull because the Navy had no time to develop its own. The result was one of the most effective and versatile craft of the Vietnam War.

sending a boarding party to inspect papers and, if the officer in charge thought necessary, search for smuggled arms.

There were few opportunities for glory or distinction out on the barrier lines. This sort of gruelling routine, aggravated by the mind-numbing repetition of searching sampans and junks with little or no result, or worse still, bobbing around the ocean when sightings were few and far between, tested the crews; but it was essential that cover was maintained. Every vessel had to be checked out, month after month, because if the Navy's vigilance slackened the enemy would be quick to notice.

VC supporters on fishing boats were watching the watchers, and would quickly detect any slackening of vigilance. An effective barrier patrol had to be just that—a permanent barrier. Conditions were not helped by the weather. Vietnam has a tropical monsoon climate with a marked typhoon season extending from July into November. During this period, the coastal winds, always changeable because of temperature variations over the land, are even more uncertain. A patrol in the South China Sea in a small ship with crowded accommodation was never a pleasure cruise.

TAKE-OFF RUN: An SP-5B Martin Marlin flying boat uses JATO (jet-assisted take-off) bottles to help it unstick from the smooth waters of Cam Ranh Bay before a Market Time surveillance flight in April 1967, the type's last year of deployment. The Marlins were finally replaced by more capable land-based planes.

The weather was a constant factor in the way resources were managed for the inshore blockade. The Swift boats could cover a patrol area more effectively, and make quicker transits to and from their stations, but only if the sea conditions allowed them to use their speed. In a storm they could not go as fast as the cutters, which were more stable in rough conditions. In a blockade an advantage in speed meant two fast boats being able to take the place of three slow ones. Speed was a "force multiplier"—saving time on the transits to and from patrol areas. Consequently, Navy commanders always considered the weather when making the most effective disposition of their forces. The result was that, with a rhythm controlled by nature, the Swift boats and the cutters were moved about according to the monsoons.

It was a consideration that, on occasion, had

significant strategic effects. When the Viet Cong launched their biggest operation of the war, the Tet Offensive of February 1968, the northeast monsoon was blowing. The 82-footers were on station off the exposed northern coast, up towards the DMZ, while the Swifts, whose speed and agility made them better suited to combat in narrow waterways, were working the gulf of Thailand in the south, and able to come quickly to the aid of the US forces fighting for the survival of South Vietnamese power in the Delta.

The effectiveness of Market Time was such a deterrent to the North Vietnamese that contacts with the enemy were few. However, during the Tet Offensive, the North Vietnamese government in Hanoi decided that one more attempt had to be made to breach the barrier. In February 1968, after a lull of more than six months, the first of five steel-hulled trawlers was spotted. It was clearly a desperate attempt to reinforce the VC forces, which were taking terrible losses, but it was doomed to fail. One trawler steamed for home when its captain realized that he had been tracked by aircraft; a second was trapped near Da Nang and scuttled by its crew; a third was blown out of the water off the Ca Mau peninsula; the fourth was caught unloading on the beach near Nha Trang and shot to pieces; and the last was seen turning and heading for home after being spotted by another aircraft. Not surprisingly it was more than a year before another trawler tried to get through again.

As the blockade's effects became noticeable, and the flow of supplies by sea began to dry up, the number of boats needed constantly on the barrier could be reduced, particularly in the daytime, when air surveillance was at its most effective. From mid-1967 onward the Swifts and Vietnamese Navy junks were regularly detailed to operate either in support of friendly troops on shore or in hit-and-run missions into VC stronghold areas to keep the Viet Cong off balance.

In one typical month of 1968, Market Time sailors took part in 860 fire support missions for forces ashore. In the same year they searched more than half a million coastal craft. The Swift crews became involved with the brown-water war even more directly during Sea Lords operations from late

Alien float —In the water it looked like driftwood topped with a tangle of palms. It was only when a PBR crew got closer that they realized that the camouflaged float in the Co Chien River carried a Viet Cong propaganda banner and a stack of anti-American leaflets.

DOUBLE WEAPON:
Swift boat machine gunners watch for the characteristic smoky impact of "Willy Pete" —white phosphorous mortar shells— before opening fire.

1968 onward, when they were asked to take over many of the inland patrol tasks of the river patrol boats in the Game Warden task force. The risks of running into a firefight were infinitely greater than they were out in the open sea, but the break from the boredom and discomfort of long patrols in bad weather and steep seas was welcomed by many. Coastal Force junks also took an increasing part in these operations.

The contrast between inshore and offshore operations was striking, as one three-boat PCF unit discovered when it was called to raid a bunker com-

plex, soon after its discovery in a side canal off the lower Bassac River in 1969.

Before the PCF raiders went in they used their 81mm mortars to bombard the target area for nearly 20 minutes. They called in air support from the Black Ponies, the Navy's close support squadron, for the dawn attack. Then the three boats entered the canal maintaining 100 yard intervals between each boat. As they travelled, they took care to spray likely looking patches of cover with machine gun fire.

The threat of ambush was greatest at the points where the banks were so narrow that both sides of

Fast-response weapon —A crewman aboard an inshore patrol boat readies his M-79 grenade launcher for action during a patrol on the Ca Mau peninsula. In an ambush the rapid-fire 40mm weapon could lob scores of grenades into a shore zone, effectively suppressing enemy fire.

the boat were brushed with creepers and the foliage plucked at the crew's helmets and flak jackets. Nor could they move at speed for fear of running aground in the winding channel. They scraped over the remains of a footbridge that had fallen into the water near an abandoned hamlet, the hootches that had once been homes, left to rot in the jungle. At times the lush green forest, dotted with brightly colored flowers, seemed completely untouched by man. They could have been in a wildlife reserve if it were not for the rattle of machine gun fire, and the rumble of the PCFs' twin diesels.

The boats began to take casualties immediately after they spotted the newly dug bunkers. Antipersonnel mines set up on the bank blasted them with shrapnel, and men in the front two boats suffered slight wounds before the order to retreat was given and an airstrike was called in. The bunkers were well camouflaged, so they were marked with smoke grenades before the PCFs pulled out. The VC in the area were now thoroughly alerted to the raiders' presence, and it was time to depart at speed. The first two boats narrowly avoided further damage when a floating mine detonated by remote control at the mouth of the side canal went off between them, but no one was hurt badly enough to require evacuation. The whole episode took less than an hour.

Similar raids into the enemy-held Ca Mau peninsula were at the beginnings of Operation Sea Float in June 1969, when a floating PCF base on barges was established near Old Nam Can, near the southernmost tip of Vietnam. This operation was part of the larger Sea Lords strategy, but it was conceived and largely carried out by Market Time units, who saw it as a way of filling the long gap between the PCF bases at Cat Lo, to the north of the Mekong delta, and An Thoi, off the Cambodian border. The canal system in the Ca Mau provided entrances and exits on both sides of the peninsula, an advantage that the waterborne forces were able to fully exploit. It was the natural theater for a classic PCF campaign of raids and incursions, backed by two strikes by heavy riverine assault craft. But that is to anticipate developments. In 1965, with Market Time running smoothly, the Navy was about to begin its fighting voyage into the delta lands of the Mekong.

Closing the
sea lanes

NIGHT MOVES:
An illumination
round from a
Swift mortar
lights up the
silhouette of
another PCF
during a support
mission for
troops in Quang
Tin province.

49

Into the Delta

Operation Game Warden

FROM THE fighting man's point of view the waterways of the Mekong Delta, which were to be the scene of the next phase of the Navy's operations, offer startling variations in terrain.

Once over the sandbars at the river mouth, the broad tributaries, several miles wide in places, flow placidly and provide a safe highway for Navy patrol boats and villagers' sampans alike. But turn off into a side channel and immediately there was danger all around. With canals as narrow as country lanes, a boat could be trapped by felling trees in front and behind it.

Most of the canals were lined with trees and brush, which provided perfect cover for ambushes, and the backdrop for a deadly game of hide-and-seek between the riverine sailors and the guerrillas.

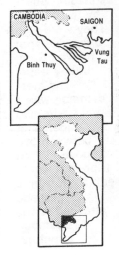

The Navy treated it as hostile territory. Before the arrival of the Game Warden forces it was estimated that 75 percent of the Mekong Delta's population was controlled or subject to intimidation by the Viet Cong.

In 1965 there were an estimated 80,000 Viet Cong and VC sympathizers in the Delta. Of these some 30,000 were thought to be regular troops and 50,000 part-time guerrillas capable of operating in battalion units.

The South Vietnamese army fielded three divisions and other units, 40,000 regular fighting men, backed up by a makeshift militia drawn from the paramilitary regional and Popular Forces.

They were losing.

A key index of Viet Cong success was the amount of rice moved in the Delta. It fell by a quarter between 1965 and 1966 as the enemy increased the amounts of rice it took as a "tax" from the

Wharf search —A sailor treads warily beneath a bamboo wharf looking for a Viet Cong arms cache. The waterside wharves were frequently used as staging posts by the enemy. They were also a favorite spot for Viet Cong booby traps. The most common was a wire tied underwater between two posts. When tripped it would pull a pin from a grenade attached to the bamboo structure.

villagers. The Vietnamese Army was reluctant to join riverine assault actions, the only way to destroy the growing enemy infrastructure of arms dumps, hideouts, and tax collectors. And without a continuous patrol force on the river, civilian traffic was at the mercy of the Viet Cong.

Before the arrival of the Black Berets, the Delta was thought of as Charlie's river, an abundant source of recruits, rice, and taxes to fuel the Viet Cong war effort. The VC, who fought out of their local villages, knew every inch of its tortuous, meandering waterways—every ambush point, every escape route.

They were a formidable foe. They had been schooled in war, first by eight years against the French and then by a decade against the nationalist regimes in Saigon, which were aided in later years by US advisors. Not all the Communist forces were equally experienced, but all were disciplined, dedicated, and possessed of formidable powers of endurance. Many were fishermen and hunters, which gave them a natural affinity for the land and water, a natural patience, and great ingenuity when it came to devising methods of killing.

The task of recapturing the waterways was assigned to Task Force 116, code named Game Warden, established on 18 December 1965. Its original mission was to patrol the inland waterways, enforce the curfew, search river traffic, and deny the Viet Cong an opportunity to infiltrate and resupply.

If the enemy was one problem, equipment was another. There was nothing in the Navy's fleet designed or equipped to do battle on the brown waters of the Delta, where the requirement was for a small, fast, shallow-draft boat capable of carrying large firepower. And there was no time to design and test a purpose-built craft. As in the case of the Market Time PCFs, a commercial boat already in production had to be modified.

The craft best suited to Navy needs was a pleasure boat built by United Boatbuilders of Bellingham, Washington, who added a naval superstructure to a standard fiberglass hull. The specifications called for the boat to be capable of 25 to 30 knots, and to draw 18 inches of water when stationary and 9 inches when cruising.

The muddy weed-clogged inland waters of South

Vietnam ruled out conventional propellor-driven propulsion. A Jacuzzi-designed system based on twin water jets was the answer. It was steered by turning the jet nozzles, so there was no rudder to become fouled. If the boat skipper wished to go astern, a U-shaped gate was dropped over the jets to reverse the flow of water.

This was the workhorse of the brown-water navy, the Mark One River Patrol Boat. Apart from a heavy complement of ordnance, about 1,000 pounds of lightweight ceramic armor—aluminum sheets sandwiched with layers of a porcelain-like material—was added to the boat, mostly around the pilothouse and gun positions.

The fiberglass hull offered a backhanded sort of protection in that the Viet Cong's main heavy ordnance, rocket-propelled grenades, went straight through without detonating their armor-piercing warhead, and what little damage was caused by these rounds could be easily repaired.

The Mark Two PBR, ordered in March 1967, was four knots faster than the Mark One, thanks to im-

CHARLIE'S VIEW:
A green-painted monitor moves into view on one of the rivers of the Mekong Delta. Most VC ambushes were close range, vicious, and short-lived affairs.

MOVING TARGETS: Three PBRs cruise an island in the Bassac River in 1967 to draw fire from suspected enemy positions. Waiting helicopter and air support would strike the targets once they were spotted.

proved jet pumps, slightly larger with the forward gun turret moved further toward the bow, and the whole boat having a slightly lower profile, making a smaller target. The hull was constructed from aluminum instead of fiberglass to reduce the fouling problems experienced by the Mark One. In the organically rich waters of the Delta, the rapid growth of marine life and the lack of time for proper maintenance meant that a hull could quickly become fouled, cutting down its speed and efficiency in the water.

The PBR's grenade launchers proved to be the most effective weapons against dug-in or hidden ambushers, as captured VC testified. The launchers lofted grenades into the air to detonate against

branches of trees, showering any sheltering VC with shrapnel. Or they could blanket an area with shards of metal when the exact position of snipers was not known. A skilled gunner could have the last grenade from a 36-round belt in the air before the first one had exploded, a daunting prospect for any Viet Cong sniper, however well dug in.

For communication, the PBRs were equipped with two AN/VRC 46 radio transmitters and, for night detection purposes, a Raytheon 1900 radar and a portable "starlight scope," which allowed the user, literally, to see in the dark.

There were drawbacks to this arsenal. The sheer power and range—more than 2,000 yards—of the .50-caliber machine gun often precluded its use on the

Seaman David G. Ouellet —saved the lives of his PBR crew when he hurled himself on a Viet Cong grenade in March 1967. Evacuated by helicopter to Saigon, he died on the operating table. He was posthumously awarded the Medal of Honor on 30 January 1968. Later a frigate was named after him.

heavily populated riverbanks. Even when there was only VC in its field of fire, the .50 was a double-edged weapon. One PBR gunner recalled: "It's difficult to be accurate with a .50 and it makes a tremendous smokescreen when firing, but it packs a great kick to it. If it hits something it will destroy it, except mud bunkers." Helicopter pilots in close support also feared the .50 because of the risk that the bullets would ricochet at all angles when they encountered a solid object.

The PBRs began operations in the Delta on 8 May 1966, when River Section 511 of River Division 51, based at Can Tho, started patrols on the Bassac River. Soon afterwards the PBRs moved into the upper Mekong and its southern arms, the My Tho, Ham Luong, and Co Chien.

The original concept of Game Warden called for groups of ten river patrol boats to work from a mixture of shore and river bases.

Four old converted tank landing ships known as APBs recommissioned in 1966 were to service the PBRs and a fire support team of two helicopters. Each section of ten boats was to be responsible for 30 miles of waterway.

Tactics were to be based on two-boat teams, commanded by a junior officer or a chief petty officer. One team patrolled during the day, three at night, while the fifth remained at base. Operating procedures were to be decided by the local situation— in other words, trial and error.

The first task was to understand the enemy's methods.

The VC sought combat only in an ambush or to divert attention away from troop movements; a convoy of enemy sampans or junks coming into contact with the heavily armed PBRs usually came off worse.

Large supply convoys or columns or troops had to be moved at night because of American air superiority. A motorized sampan could power through the water at 30 knots. So Charlie waited for the first PBR to pass, then darted out a creek on one side of the river to safety on the other bank. The flat Delta area provided excellent staging posts and the seemingly endless lines of trees on the river and canal banks provided ambush points.

At first the Viet Cong found it easy to elude the

patrolling PBRs; they were few and far between. The black pajama-clad guerrillas crouched in the undergrowth and tree lines and just waited for an opportunity to pounce or slip away when the patrol boats passed.

The most effective tactics were those of deception and stealth, and an enemy waiting in silence had the advantage over the crews of the diesel-engined PBRs. Although a Viet Cong guerrilla's individual armory was restricted to what he could carry, he could still pack a considerable fighting punch.

The most common weapons were recoilless rifles, rocket-propelled grenades (the B-40 and more feared B-41), and the sturdy and reliable AK-47 automatic rifle.

All these weapons were usually fired at extremely close range, although the B-40 had an effective

SURFING ALONG: A PBR captain scans the river-bank looking for hidden enemy positions. Crews had to be on constant alert for ambushes, rocket fire, and tossed grenades. But the PBRs were not easy targets with their profile and quick acceleration.

range of about 120 meters and the 57mm recoilless rifles, with their smaller charge, had one of about 1,000 meters.

The Americans responded swiftly to the enemy tactics. To be successful they had to learn to fight the Viet Cong way, on the Viet Cong's terms. "Ambush or be ambushed" was the law of this waterlogged jungle.

It was like a game of chess played with live pieces. Both sides knew the board and thought they knew the moves that could be made, but both could make mistakes or spring lethal surprises.

Seasoned players describe their techniques and

some of the problems: "How do you go about selecting a site for an ambush? If you have real-time intelligence of enemy movement through your area the process is simple. You choose a site athwart the enemy's route where the concealment factor is good and your field of fire is as unrestricted as possible. However, you are seldom fortunate enough to have such intelligence.

"The process then becomes something not unlike a game of chess played with a clever opponent. Having studied the river very carefully, both you and the enemy know where the best crossings are. You have both examined minutely the pattern of the

POWERING ALONG: A Mark Two PBR makes a high-speed run along the Long Tau River, the main shipping channel from Saigon to the sea. The water jet propulsion system delivered up to 30 knots and a draft of 9 inches, giving great speed and maneuverability on the shallow rivers.

other's behaviour. The final stage in the process then becomes nothing more or less than an attempt to outwit or outguess." Another American river fighter recalled the constant anticipation of danger: "It's good out there because you know where you're going. You make the turn off the big river, where no one bothers you, into a canal you know you're going to get ambushed—because it happens so many times.

"In eight months I went on over 60 operations and got ambushed 20 times, not a very good average. It's hard to tell most of the time who your enemy is, because a man can be standing out in a field waving to you that day, and then you'll draw sniper fire from the same place that night."

In a situation where wits needed to be at their sharpest, crews were also constantly fatigued. They usually worked 80- to 90-hour weeks, half at night, and even on so-called rest days the boats had to be cleaned, refueled, and repaired. Sleep had to be snatched in temperatures in the hundreds.

Daytime patrols were spent checking the never-ending stream of junks and sampans moving along the Mekong. Ninety percent of a skipper's time was spent waiting for things to happen or checking cargo manifests, checking holds to see if their contents tallied, probing under the cargo to see whether weapons or money were hidden and checking identification cards. The lack of one, or a forged one, indicated a draft dodger or VC supporter. PBRs usually carried a Vietnamese national policeman to spot forgeries and provide interpretation.

During the days the boats steamed in open column, with a "lead" boat about 400 to 600 yards in front of the "cover" boat. The gap between them was important. It meant that both would be unlikely to be caught in the same ambush, but they were close enough for their radar coverage and weapon range to overlap and to prevent an enemy craft sneaking between them. At nights they drifted silently with the stream, anchored, or used a quiet outboard motor. Only when the enemy were engaged did the boat captain hit full throttle.

On patrol the PBR crews never knew when they would be hit next. One PBR crew man described how the first move always belonged to the Viet Cong:

Boatswain's Mate First Class James E. Williams —awarded the Medal of Honor for decisive leadership, initiative, and courage during an action in which two PBRs under his command destroyed 65 enemy boats in a supply convoy.

> They've got to initiate the firefight because we couldn't see them. But it only took a matter of two seconds to start firing your weapon and usually when the VC hit us, maybe their first two or three rockets would be on target and the rest would go wide, or high or low—for the simple reason that as soon as they exposed themselves they were in trouble.
> They couldn't afford to stand up because when a column of boats opens up, in theory, there's about five guns working on each boat. If I jumped up and saw just one boat with two .50s and two .20s looking at me I don't think I'd jump up too often. Out of all the firefights I've been in I've only seen the Viet Cong once. He was behind a bunker and he decided to get up and run which was not a very good idea because he didn't get more than two feet."

When the boats' firepower was combined with the blazing guns of choppers any Viet Cong caught in

Into the Delta

SHARK'S TEETH: A Navy Patrol Air Cushion Vehicle (PACV), hovers along the My Tho River in 1967. Faster, noisier, and less maneuverable than PBRs, the PACVs were used on wider rivers, bays, and swamps where speed was critical. A PACV could drive right over riverbanks and dykes to chase the enemy, to whom they made a monstrous sight with their shark's teeth bow, howling engine and .50-caliber machine guns and 40mm cannons. (PACV crews adopted the call sign ''Monster''.) Against their widespread introduction was cost: A PACV sold for nearly $1 million, a PBR for $90,000.

the cross fire seldom survived. "We had Cobras a lot of the time but most of the time we had Sea Wolves. I'll never forget when a Cobra opened up with a minigun on a tree line, it looked almost like a lawnmower took to the trees, cut them all down."

The original requirement had been for 80 PBRs to pacify the Delta, plus a further 40 in the Rung Sat, an ancient pirates' haven known as "The Forest of Assassins" consisting of a 20-square-mile maze of channels through thickly growing mangrove and

nipa swamp lying on the strategically vital route
between Saigon and the sea. But it was very soon
apparent that the task force commander's resources
were stretched far too thin. It took all his forces to
react to enemy action, leaving nothing to seize the
initiative. Forty extra PBRs were ordered in 1966
and by 1967 the total had risen to 155, with 30
stationed in the Rung Sat. Even that number was
sufficient only to scratch the surface of enemy
activity. In February, a force of 250 PBRs was

Primitive but effective —Two Viet Cong mines of a type detonated by remote control through a wire onto the river or canal bank. The counter to this type of mine was a chain drag to break the wire. Underwater mines were a riverine weapon that the Viet Cong never fully exploited, fearing that their own boats might fall victim.

approved and a new task force, 117, later to be known as the Mobile Riverine Force (MRF), was established to undertake more aggressive search-and-destroy actions with the Army.

In 1967, Game Warden forces boarded 400,000 vessels in the unceasing search for enemy contraband and infiltrators. One PBR could easily check around 300 sampans during the morning "rush hour." Most searches were frustrating, turning up nothing. The nights were a different story, though.

The River Patrol Force's tally for 1967 was 2,000 Viet Cong craft destroyed, damaged, or captured; and more than 1,400 of the enemy killed, captured, or wounded at a cost of 39 officers and men killed, 366 wounded, and nine missing.

In 1968, as the ever-expanding American forces took a tighter grip on the Delta, Game Warden and Task Force 116 were subdivided into four groups. River Patrol Task Force group commands were established on the Co Chien, My Tho, Bassac, and in the Rung Sat. In that year the PBR total reached 250, although 20 were hived off into a self-contained task force, Clearwater, to operate in the I Corps area up near the DMZ and the border with North Vietnam.

THE STORY of the PBRs is more than just statistics. It is a human one. The young sailors who took on and beat Charlie in his own territory and on his own short-range terms formed a force without precedent in the US Navy.

Their courage and team spirit are reflected in the fact that the PBR crews were the most decorated naval command of the war.

And despite the dangerous, uncomfortable, and demanding working conditions, a fifth of PBR crewmen requested a six-month extension of duty in Vietnam where one in three could expect to be wounded.

The key to these testimonials of dedication to duty lay in the close comradeship and enormous responsibility thrust on the sailors who adopted the black beret as their symbol.

Each PBR had a crew of four, with the captain usually of the rank of petty officer first class. The crew was comprised of a gunner's mate, engineman, and seaman — but in a firefight everyone manned a gun except the man at the wheel. In addition, everyone was trained to pilot and navigate the boat, operate the electronics, maintain the engine, and fire all the weapons.

All these factors combined to put enormous demands and responsibility on the shoulders of the bluejackets, especially the boat captain. In return they were given an unparalleled opportunity to lead men and make decisions about how they fought. The sort of decisions a boatswain's mate could take on a PBR would be a Captain's responsibility on a destroyer.

And few destroyer captains had the chance in Vietnam to show the daring of the men of the PBRs.

Take the incident that occurred late in the afternoon of 31 October 1966, when two PBRs from River Section 531 under the command of James E. Williams, boatswain's mate first class, suddenly came under fire from two sampans on the Nam Thon branch of the Mekong River. The boats returned fire with a vengeance, sinking one sampan and chasing the other up an inlet, where they were then fired on by two concealed junks and eight more sampans and fortified positions along the bank. Williams had stumbled across a major VC supply convoy and a crossing attempt by three heavy weapons companies

CLEAN SWEEP: Crewmen on a PACV preparing to embark captured VC during an operation near Moc Hoa in the Plain of Reeds, a swamp 70 miles long and 30 miles wide near the Cambodian border used by the VC for rest and training.

totalling nearly 400 men. After calling up artillery
and air strikes—Williams greeted the lead helicopter
with the remark "I want y'all to go in there and hold
field day on them guys"—the boats returned to the
attack, discovering even more concealed enemy
craft. Disregarding blistering automatic weapon
fire, in which Williams was wounded, Williams'
team damaged or destroyed another seven junks and
50 sampans. As darkness fell the fighting was still
heavy. He ordered the boat's searchlights to be swit-
ched on, despite the dangers of giving away his position, and moved closer to the shore, pouring out lead
onto the numerically superior VC forces. They soon
broke and fled.

The three-hour action cost the enemy 65 boats, 16

deaths, 24 wounded, and the loss of 2,400 pounds of rice — a week's rations for a battalion. Petty Officer Williams was awarded the Medal of Honor for his decisive leadership, initiative, and courage.

In cold statistical staff officer terms, Game Warden crews logged up 70,000 patrol hours in an average month, the Sea Wolves flew some 1,500 support missions, while the Seals, the Navy's special warfare unit, made 60 forays. Minesweeping patrols totalled 75, while LSTs engaged in 20 gunfire support missions—with PBRs and helicopters being involved in about 80 firefights a month. Helicopter gunship support was considered vital when Game Warden's mission was drawn up in the winter of 1966, but the Navy had no helicopter gunships and its anti-

THREE OF A KIND: PACVs chasing Charlie, sweeping from water to swamp to solid ground without even slowing down. The Bell PACV could skim on a 4-foot bubble of air at 60 knots powered by a gas turbine engine.

Mine detector —Crewmen aboard a US Navy minesweeping boat (MSB) prepare to rig a paravane buoy for a minesweeping exercise in the Long Tau River. As the buoy was towed, the fins stabilized it at a safe distance from the MSB. The buoy floated deep enough for its towing wire to cut through the cables that anchored enemy mines to the bottom of the river. Once they had floated to the surface, these mines were usually detonated by machine gun and cannon fire.

submarine warfare (ASM) machines were too heavy, large, and expensive to be adapted to the role. The Army, which was successfully using Bell UH-1 Iroquois gunships, was given the role of providing air support, with the first two of these Hueys arriving in March 1966 even before the first PBRs. By the end of the year Game Warden was operating eight of the Army Hueys.

In April 1967 the Navy's Helicopter Attack (Light) Squadron Three, to be known as HAL-3 was commissioned. By September it comprised 14 Hueys divided into seven fire teams plus a pool of eight at the maintenance base at Vung Tau.

HAL-3 adopted the call sign of "Sea Wolves" and the black beret.

On combat missions their Hueys flew in pairs, with the lead aircraft flying about 100 feet higher so the one behind could unleash supporting fire underneath. They patrolled at about 1,200 feet. Flying at treetop level, as well as being physically demanding and dangerous, made the Sea Wolves too vulnerable to small-arms fire and reduced their field of vision.

The crews were kept on 24-hour alert and could be scrambled in three minutes night or day from the PBR bases. They were never usually more than 15 minutes' flying time from boats that had requested assistance. When not on alert the Hueys flew reconnaissance patrols and supported planned Game Warden operations.

A Huey crew consisted of a pilot, copilot, and two door gunners, each equipped with a .50-cal machine gun that could be fired through a 180-degree arc. The armament consisted of seven forward-firing 2.75-inch rockets and fixed 7.62mm machine guns mounted over the rocket packs. Their maximum combat speed was about 90 knots, with a patrol capability of around 90 minutes. The frightening array of rockets and machine guns was enhanced by the wolf painted on their noses. But the Sea Wolves were always stretched too thin. The Navy's quota of aircraft was raised to 33 in April 1969 only after the Army had taken delivery of the new Cobra (AH-1G) gunships.

However, that month Game Warden received more air firepower in the form of 16 OV-10 Broncos, a fixed-wing short take-off-and-landing (Stol) air-

craft. Eight were stationed at Vung Tau and the rest at Binh Thuy, from where they covered the whole of the Delta and Rung Sat. Their call sign and nickname was the Black Ponies.

The Bronco was a light but rugged two-seater reconnaissance plane designed for counter-insurgency operations. Armed with machine guns, bombs, rockets, and missiles, it had a top speed of 305 knots—twice that of a helicopter—and a payload of 2,400 pounds. But what the Bronco made up in extra firepower because of its greater weight, it lost

CHANNEL SWEEP:
A minesweeping boat patrols the Long Tau River below Saigon, number one target for VC saboteurs. Davits on the stern were used to control sweep wires.

in mobility. Although it needed only 1,130 feet of runway, it could not operate from the mobile PBR bases as could the helicopters.

Also Broncos lacked the maneuverability and accuracy of the Huey over a target. But on the plus side it could absorb much more hostile fire and the sheer destructiveness of the Broncos' Zuni rockets won many friends among the river boat crews.

The muddy brown waters of Vietnam also hid another potential killer—mines. Usually they were free-floating or command-detonated after being fastened by swimmers or anchored in busy channels,

in particular the Long Tau leading to Saigon, and the Cua Viet and Perfume rivers. The simple solution employed on the Long Tau was defoliation of the banks, which destroyed Charlie's cover and made command detonation extremely hazardous. So he had to retreat further and further inland, making mining, apart from swimmer-borne limpet mines, much less successful.

However, floating mines were always a threat. The simple and often very effective solution adopted by the boat crews was to hurl grenades at any suspicious-looking object. Mining the waterways was

OPERATION FLAMING ARROW: LCDR Donald D. Sheppard uses a longbow and arrow to set alight a bamboo hut concealing a fortified VC bunker near the Bassac River in November 1967.

Into the Delta

MORNING RUSH HOUR:
A PBR takes evasive action to avoid heavy boat traffic. Rivers were used as roads in South Vietnam. Yet every sampan and junk could conceal VC men or supplies. A large and unglamorous part of the PBR crew's job was checking river traffic. It was not unusual for one PBR crew to check 300 sampans and junks in the space of a morning.

also part of the Viet Cong's propaganda war, giving the impression of an enemy that could strike anywhere when the reality was that these attacks scored few direct hits and did little damage.

But had a large ship been sunk on the narrow Long Tau or Cua Viet, both vital for the logistical war effort, the channel would have taken weeks to clear.

The Cua Viet and Perfume rivers were only about 12 to 15 feet deep at best, whereas the Long Tau, My Tho, and Bassac rivers ranged from 30 to 60 feet deep. The main task of keeping the rivers clear fell

to the wooden-hulled 57-foot minesweeping boats (MSBs), which weighed 41 tons and were capable of 14 knots.

In 1968, after being awarded the Presidential Unit Citation, Mine Squadron 11 was renamed Mine Division 112 and equipped with six MSBs and five river minesweepers (MSMs) built on LCM (6) hulls. Later that year Mine Division 113 was commissioned to increase coverage on the Rung Sat and a detachment to sweep Da Nang harbor in I Corps. Four MSMs were also sent to the Perfume River and five to the Cua Viet River.

The deadly elite

THE TOUGHEST of the Navy's riverine forces were the Seals, commandos whose name was devised from the opening letters of the theaters they trained to fight in: Sea, Air, and Land.

Although the Seals' total strength in Vietnam throughout the war never exceeded 200, their impact was enormous. Seal Teams One and Two had been commissioned by President John Kennedy on 1 January 1962 as highly skilled, lightly armed forces operating in small teams that could be effective where conventional units could not—deep inside enemy territory.

They were first deployed in Vietnam that year, and started a training program for South Vietnamese Marines. From 1964 on a Seal team was involved in covert special operations from a base near Da Nang, close to the DMZ and the North Vietnamese border.

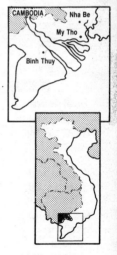

The Seals, who served with the Game Warden forces from February 1966 on, were trained in hand-to-hand combat, scuba diving, underwater demolition, and parachuting. They were proficient with a wide variety of weapons and could speak several local languages. They were also expert in survival, evasion, and escape.

Such an elite force was only deployed selectively; Seals' targets were usually intelligence objectives of high value that could not be reached by conventional means.

Sometimes the targets were places, sometimes they were people. A classic example unfolded in the bay of Nha Trang in March 1969, when Lieutenant (j.g.) Joseph R. Kerrey and his five-man Seal team were landed on an island—known to be a well-defended VC sanctuary. The island was home to

A Seal team on a strike assault boat on a high-speed patrol near the Cambodian border in 1970. The STAB is armed with M-60 machine guns and a 40mm automatic grenade launcher.

several important members of the Viet Cong's area political cadre (the senior officers of the district). The VC officers would be a rich source of intelligence. If they could be interrogated vital intelligence would be gained. Lieutenant Kerrey's mission was to penetrate the enemy's defenses and bring back the VC officers—alive.

The VC camp was almost impregnable, located on a large ledge halfway down a 350-foot sheer cliff. Any direct approach from below was tempting suicide, straight into the gaze of the enemy gunners, so Lieutenant Kerrey decided to scale the cliff first, and descend on the enemy from the least likely direction—above.

The operation went almost according to plan. Kerrey split his team into 2 three-man sections, and coordinated the nerve-racking climb down the treacherous cliff with whispered instructions on the radio. To fall, or even drop an item of equipment, would mean detection and death for the entire team.

The two groups were only feet from their objective when Kerrey's group was spotted and instantly blasted with fire. Kerrey was seriously wounded by a grenade that landed at his feet. But it was too late for the attack to be thwarted. The wounded Kerrey ordered the other group to open fire, and the surprise cross fire soon silenced the enemy gunners.

The VIP prisoners secured, Kerrey, who won the Congressional Medal of Honor for this exploit, remained in cool control, first selecting a suitable site to call in the extraction helicopters and then organizing its defense.

The first two Seal platoons operating with the Game Warden forces were sent into the Rung Sat Special Zone to disrupt enemy sappers' attempts to mine allied shipping. Later on, the Seals were used to infiltrate enemy territory and carry out hit-and-run raids, almost always at night. They were usually "inserted" and collected by a Mike boat, an armored craft, or the faster but more lightly armored

Lieutenant Joseph R. Kerrey —awarded the Medal of Honor after he was injured in a daring cliff-scaling assault on a Viet Cong stronghold.

PBR. As they refined their tactics, and more equipment became available, Seals used light, fast Boston Whalers, Seal Team Assault Boats (Stabs) and Light Seal Support Craft (LSSCs). But when they needed to go in deeper enemy-held territory disguised as fishermen, they used sampans. The Stab boat, similar to the Boston whaler and powered by an outboard motor, was phased out with the arrival of the LSSC in July 1968.

The 24-foot-long aluminium LSSC was well suited to inshore operations. With a low silhouette that made it difficult to spot and propulsion by a Jacuzzi water jet pump at more than 30 knots, it was a match for any enemy sampan that tried to make a dash for safety.

The initial success of the Seals in the Rung Sat led to the deployment of four more platoons to South Vietnam. Two were sent to Nha Be, one to Binh Thuy, and one to My Tho. Although their main function continued to be small-unit raids in enemy territory, usually operating in six-man squads, they were also used to spearhead river operations in the Delta and as reconnaissance patrols for larger units. In some joint operations they linked up with the Green Berets, their Army counterparts.

As part of their deep-cover intelligence role, the commandos would lie hidden on riverbanks and canals away from the main rivers where the Viet Cong were accustomed to move with impunity, watching and waiting to discover which were the enemy supply routes.

By early 1967 the Seals had gained a reputation of getting results, which led to more and more requests for their services from area commanders. The Seals' periods of duty on listening post and ambush operations were extended to seven days without resupply, which gave a better perspective of VC operations and enabled more effective ambushes to be plotted. By 1968 the Seals began operating as advisors to US and Vietnamese forces, training them in the tactics of counterguerrilla warfare. Even while the rest of the American forces were being scaled down, the number of Navy commandos was increasing. Late in 1969 Seal Team Two received two additional platoons and it was only in 1970 that they began turning over their duties to their Vietnamese counterparts. In one action late in 1970 the Seals teamed up with South Vietnamese militiamen to raid a VC prison camp and rescued 19 South Vietnamese, captured 2 VC, and seized documents and weapons.

In 1972 the number of Seals serving in Vietnam was reduced drastically, though a few remained behind in South Vietnam as advisors until the end of the war, two years later.

Typical of their heroism was the actions of Robert T. Gallagher, a senior chief petty officer serving with the Seal Team Detachment Alpha on 13 March 1968.

Gallagher was the assistant patrol leader on a night mission deep into an enemy battalion base area. His patrol had penetrated 5,000 yards into the Viet Cong base camp area without incident when they came across a barracks occupied by about 30 heavily armed VC. Gallagher and three other men went into the barracks, but were fired on by a sentry.

In the firefight that followed, Gallagher was wounded in both legs but still accounted for five dead VC.

His patrol leader was even more seriously hurt, forcing Gallagher to take command of the heavily outnumbered and outgunned team. Gallagher led them through the darkness and 1,000 yards of enemy territory before he thought it safe to call up helicopter support.

When the choppers arrived Gallagher risked his life, constantly exposing himself to heavy enemy automatic fire, as he directed gunships and extraction choppers. Although wounded a second time, Gallagher continued to oversee the successful evacuation of his Seal team.

The courage and initiative that was the trademark of the Seals won him the Navy Cross.

The Seals could be as controversial as they were courageous. One politically sensitive area of operations was the Phoenix program, in which Seals worked with South Vietnamese Provincial Reconnaissance Units, whose job was to kill or capture VC leaders or political officers.

By eliminating the commanders of the VC, many attacks were nipped in the bud. But back in the States, where the antiwar movement was gathering momentum, the program was political dynamite, denounced as akin to "murder for hire" by the war

Lt. Thomas R. Norris —awarded the Medal of Honor for his "decisive leadership, undaunted courage, and selfless dedication" as he led a Seal mission into enemy territory to rescue two downed American fliers. After rescuing one, Norris returned to find and rescue the other. Travelling in a sampan, disguised as a fisherman, Norris found the injured man and hid him under a pile of bamboo for the boat journey back. On the way Norris dodged an NVA patrol, and called in an air strike on an enemy machine gun nest.

protestors. In six years the tiny band of Seals accounted for 600 confirmed VC killed, 300 almost certainly killed, captured or detained, at a cost of less than a dozen Seals casualties.

No statistical tally can be placed on the effects of the intelligence they gathered. But it made a contribution to the war out of all proportion to their numbers. In the psychological war too they came out winners, going some way towards evening up the unspoken balance of terror, and gaining a reputation as fearsome and extraordinary soldiers.

The most extraordinary among them was, indeed,

The deadly elite

TAKING OUT CHARLIE:
Seals carrying an assortment of weapons go ashore from an Assault River Patrol Boat beached along the Rach Mo canal 50 miles south-west of Saigon to destroy a VC base with about 50 bunkers.

not human; he was Prince, a German shepherd dog trained to parachute.

One of his uses was as an interrogation aid, tearing the clothes off terrified VC prisoners to loosen their tongues. One night during an incursion in the Delta the dog was wounded, but he recovered and was awarded the Purple Heart.

Most Seal operations remain classified, shrouded in secrecy, or lost in the mists of time. But one member of the Australians' Special Air Service,—no mean achievers themselves—who served with the Seals summed up them up as "The best, bar none."

Strike force

EARLY ON, the South Vietnamese government had been reluctant to have US combat forces deployed in IV Corps, the Delta area. But the Game Warden patrols had shown that it was too important and too close to being lost completely to be left to the ARVN and the Vietnamese Navy to defend. Consequently, in July 1966, US Defense Secretary Robert McNamara gave his approval to the creation of a joint Army/Navy Mobile Riverine Force (MRF) designed to take the fight to the enemy and destroy him—a much more aggressive concept than the Market Time patrol. The new force would follow the example of the French and South Vietnamese naval assault divisions, although on a larger scale.

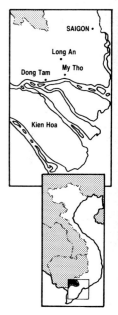

The Marines were the obvious choice to provide the troop component of the MRF, but in 1966 they were already too heavily committed far to the north in I Corps. So the honor fell to the 2nd Brigade of the US Army's 9th Infantry Division, which after saying good-bye to its tanks, trucks, armored personnel carriers, and jeeps set off for South Vietnam for training in the use of those vehicles' waterborne equivalents.

The operational plan for the MRF called for troops to be transported to the area of operations, put ashore by armored landing craft, and given fire support by special heavily armed craft and their own artillery units, which would move and fight on water.

By June 1968, two brigades of the 9th Infantry Division were deployed in the Delta, each with a supporting battalion of artillery. Each brigade operated with two River Assault Squadrons of some 50 armored craft, the squadrons in turn being split into two River Assault Divisions, each manned by 200 Black Berets. On 28 February 1967, the Riverine

Strike force

MOTHER SHIP: Monitors and ATC(H)s of an MRF division tied up alongside the self-propelled barracks ship *Benewah* (APB-35) in the Soi Rap River in the Rung Sat Special Zone. The *Benewah*, a World War II vessel updated for use in Vietnam, provided air-conditioned quarters for around 500 soldiers and sailors. It was also equipped as the command control flagship for an infantry brigade.

Assault Force, Task Force 117, was activated under the command of Naval Forces, Vietnam. In April the support ships *Kemper County* (LST 854), *Benewah* (APB 35), and *Colleton* (APB 36) moved into position. By mid-June the last LCM landing craft had arrived and the MRF was operational. The provision of only three self-propelled barracks ships (APBs) instead of the five requested meant that one battalion of the three in the 2nd Brigade had at first to operate from newly constructed shore facilities at Dong Tam,

on the northernmost branch of the Mekong. This was the MRF's land base. It provided heavy repair facilities for the naval element, an airstrip, and a little piece of dry land for the infantrymen.

For combat purposes, however, the MRF operated from a Mobile Riverine Base (MRB) usually comprising ten ships. Normally one or two infantry battalions and one River Assault Squadron would use one floating base. The makeup of an MRB varied according to the forces available. Typically

TANGO BOAT:
A purple smoke flare marks an already secure jungle landing point for an ATC, giving the crew time to unbatten the ramp of the blunt-bowed ATC, known as a Tango boat, after its call sign.

it would include two barracks/headquarters ships and a non-self-propelled barracks barge, two LST landing ships used for stores transport, a landing craft repair ship, a multipurpose berthing/mess-hall barge, two large harbor tugs, and a net-laying ship to prepare antisaboteur defenses.

The main MRF boats were all conversions of the 60-foot-long LCM(6) landing craft, which itself saw no significant service during the Vietnam War.

The workhorse of the MRF was the armored troop carrier (ATC). Each squadron had 26, with two others converted as refuelers. They were protected by stand-off armor, and a framework of iron bars set approximately 12 inches outside the hull and superstructure, designed to foil and detonate RPG or recoilless rocket rounds before they hit the main boat armor. This unusual structure allowed air to flow through the boat, as well as having the advantage of lightness.

The blunt-bowed ATC was used to land—"insert"—troops, resupply them, and provide close-in fire support. Known as a "tango boat," the ATC with its square bow and slow speed cut a less than glorious figure as it travelled through the water. Contrasted to the PBR, it threw up less wake and tended to get ignored when it came to sending publicity shots of the riverine war back to the States. Yet the crews of the ATCs were just as much in the thick of combat as those on the PBRs, and their achievements were well regarded by other riverine fighters.

Some armored troop carriers were also modified into the ATC (H) to take a helicopter flight deck over the troop well, principally for casualty evacuation. In turn some ATC (H)s were converted into battalion aid stations, with refrigerated blood supply, a surgeon, and corpsmen.

The main fire support vessel was the heavily armed and armored Monitor. This modified LCM (6) was given a spoon bow for streamlining purposes, but was so heavily armored that it weighed 75 tons. The Monitors were expected to go within feet of a hostile shore to provide support to landed infantry. Each River Assault Squadron deployed five Monitors. Two were also equipped as Command Control Boats (CCBs).

The one boat specifically designed and constructed for the MRF was the Armored Support Patrol Boat (ASPB), designed to perform the same river patrol duties as the Monitor, but a few knots faster.

ASPBs were also used as minesweepers, fitted with chain drags to snag the command wires to mines. The ASPB's special exhaust system made it the quietest river boat, although propeller-driven. It was an ideal choice for night ambushes, special operations, and night patrols. Each squadron was equipped with 16 ASPBs, 8 per division.

One of the most remarkable pieces of improvisation in the riverine war was the floating artillery barge, specially developed to meet the MRF's need for mobile fire support. Various pontoon combinations were tried before the staff of the 34th Artillery regiment hit on a method of constructing a barge out of standard 7- by 5-foot navy pontoons.

Each barge carried two 105mm howitzers, with

Evil beware —The eyes of a Yabuta junk stare fixedly ahead from a newly finished junk in a boatyard. According to a centuries-old Vietnamese belief the eyes warded off evil spirits. The South Vietnamese who sailed these coastal patrol vessels needed all the help they could get. Unlike the US patrol boats the Yabuta junks were not armed. The only weapons were the pistols and rifles of the crew.

Strike force

MONITOR IN THE MEKONG:

The 60-foot spoon-bowed Monitor was the battleship of the Mobile Riverine Force serving as a close-inshore fire support vessel. It was so heavily armed that it displaced 75 tons and had a maximum speed of 8 knots. The turret housed a 40mm cannon plus a .50-cal machine gun. Other armaments on the twin-screw diesel-powered boat included an 81mm mortar in a hybrid mount with a .50-cal machine gun, one 20mm cannon, four .30-cal machine guns, and two grenade launchers.

three barges to a battery. Maneuvering a three-barge battery into action required a total of five LCM (8) landing craft, which between them would also house the command center and ammunition supply. Once towed into position, the barges were moored to the riverbank before their artillery pieces could be fired.

Air support, a vital component in the MRF's effectiveness, was provided on a routine basis for the 2nd Brigade from the 9th Division's parent assets. An infantry battalion on an operation was normally allocated five transport and two gunfire helicopters for ten hours per day. At least one of these was used to resupply and reposition scattered

units while the rest were engaged in tactical troop movements, reconnaissance, laying ambushes, positioning patrols, and other combat-related tasks only possible by helicopter.

Although the boats of the MRF did provide great mobility and firepower, the American riverine forces would have been much less decisive without the sustained firepower of the field artillery barges and, above all, the versatility of the helicopter.

The riverine forces had no established military doctrine to fight by. There was the rather limited experience of the underequipped French to follow which had been borne out by the ineffectiveness of the South Vietnamese in preventing waterborne

Loading up —A US Navy doorgunner loads a cartridge belt of machine gun ammo into the flexible ammunition feed chute of his M-60 flex gun. Note the survival knife and .45 bullets in his belt. Inside his flak jacket is a survival radio. In the event of being shot down this would be his only link with his rescuers.

enemy incursions. There was also the division of responsibility between the Army and Navy to settle.

The Army took responsibility for the conduct of tactical operations, defense of afloat bases, co-ordination of supporting fire, and liaison with Viet-namese authorities. The Navy was in charge of the support for Army operations, assistance in the defense of bases, escorting all waterborne movements, and providing logistic support.

These command divisions proved flexible in action and in general worked well as the Army and Navy soon mastered the novel tactics needed to fight and win a guerrilla war.

Riverine commanders defined their job as "to find the VC, fix 'em, and defeat 'em." Tactical surprise was vital, the enemy had to be cornered and forced to fight. The VC would always try to elude and escape superior allied forces. Only by destroying Communist forces on the ground and driving them out of strongholds could the Delta be reclaimed for the Saigon government, whose troops joined many of the MRF operations.

Individual MRF assignments were always dif-ferent, but they all followed the same preliminary pattern. The day before the operation was spent checking boats, equipment, and guns, and topping up with fuel and ammunition. In the evening, boat captains were briefed on the next day's mission, in-cluding steaming formations, radio codes, loading orders, movement plans, and the latest intelligence on the enemy. The captains then returned to their boats to brief their crews.

A final review of the checklists was followed by an all-too-short few hours of sleep.

It was still dark when the crews stumbled to a quick breakfast on the MRB. Shortly afterwards the sounds of the night were lost in the starting of the engines. The boats cast off lines and moved away from the base ship to cruise slowly in a circle nearby.

At the appointed time, three ATCs broke off to em-bark the infantry waiting on a pontoon pier before rejoining the steaming circle.

Finally, the monitors and CCBs came alongside to pick up the command groups.

The ASPBs moved off into the dawn mist on signal. The ATCs, Monitors, and CCBs followed in

the prescribed sequence. The infantry, who had also spent the previous day checking equipment and receiving orders, settled into the cramped quarters of the boat and tried to catch up on their sleep.

But this quiet period seldom lasted long. As soon as VC country was reached or when the course followed a narrow waterway, the boat crews went to general quarters. Helicopters arrived overhead to scout the riverbanks and bends ahead for signs of the enemy. Soon afterwards the Monitors began to fire on possible enemy positions or weapons emplacements, under control of the division commanders. Then as the landing site was approached, the thunder of artillery and air strikes were added to the rattle of boat guns in the final preparation for the landing assault.

When the troop-carrying column of ATCs arrived abreast of the landing site, the signal was given for the boats to turn toward the shore. At the same time the Monitors maneuvered to the perimeter of the landing area and continued to pour suppressive fire into known or suspected enemy positions to keep the

RIVERINE SPECIAL: **An Assault Support Boat (ASPB) of the Mobile Riverine Force patrols a Delta canal as a Chinook helicopter removes equipment from a temporary fire support base. The ASPB was the only boat to be purpose-built for the MRF. Lighter and faster than the Monitor, it was used as a patrol vessel and minesweeper.**

VC gunners' heads down while the ASPBs moved to cover the opposite banks of the waterway and the flanks of the formation.

On beaching, the ATCs dropped their ramps and the troops stepped off into the lonely, dirty, and danger-filled world of the combat infantryman. While the infantrymen spread out into line, or dashed for a key blocking position, searching for the elusive enemy, the boats moved to prevent the enemy escaping over water, provide supporting fire or picking up troops for a tactical maneuver.

When the battle began ashore, the wounded were

brought to the aid boat for initial treatment and evacuation by helicopter. Supply ATCs brought more rations, water, and ammunition. Such actions could last three days until, at last, the operation was over, the enemy dead counted, and the bone-weary, mud-encrusted soldiers re-embarked for the return to base. . . and the hard-earned hot showers, hot chow, and air-conditioned bunks.

The greatest obstacle to prolonged infantry operations was not the enemy but "immersion foot," a painful crippling condition that set in after about two days of wading in constant mud and water. After three days troops had to be withdrawn.

Lifting troops out of an operations zone was one of the most hazardous parts of an MRF operation. At the best of times it could be tricky for an infantry unit to break contact with the enemy, and the situation was complicated by the need to load units onto the troop carriers. If things began to go wrong, decisive, sometimes heroic action was needed to avert disaster.

On the afternoon of 15 June 1969, Lieutenant Thomas G. Kelley was commanding River Assault Division 152 during the extraction of an infantry company from the east bank of a canal in Kien Hoa province, in the northeastern part of the Delta, a VC stronghold area.

The column of eight river assault craft had moved in to the extraction point without mishap, and the first craft were pulling off the bank with their load when one of the Armored Troop Carriers reported that the power-driven loading ramp had failed.

Almost at once heavy VC fire erupted from the

opposite bank of the canal. Ambush! Lieutenant Kelley reacted quickly, ordering the commander of the crippled craft to start raising the ramp by hand, and deploying the remaining boats in a half-circle around it to shelter the men working on the ramp from enemy fire.

While the ramp was under repair Kelley's unit was in increasing danger, and the only solution was to slug it out with the VC ambushers. Kelley as commanding officer maneuvered his command Monitor to the exposed side of the protective ring, closest to the enemy gunners, and into the heart of the action. As the CCB's guns opened up on the enemy positions a rocket-propelled grenade scored a direct hit, penetrating the armor and spraying the interior with shrapnel. Lieutenant Kelley was hurled to the deck with serious head wounds.

With the commander wounded, the situation for Assault Division 152, pinned down by enemy fire, was rapidly deteriorating.

Lieutenant Kelley was so badly injured that he could not use the radio, but he kept on directing the battle. One of his men relayed his commands to the other monitors, to such effect that they succeeded in silencing the enemy, and the entire unit was able to withdraw. For his courage and determination to bring his unit through despite his wounds, Lieutenant Kelley was awarded the Medal of Honor.

Armored troop carriers lining up to bring elements of the 9th Infantry Division ashore. Awnings protected the troops from the sun and rain and the bow ramp lowered to allow disembarkation.

The assault operations of the MRF lasted from mid-1967 to mid-1969, the first eight months being spent in search-and-destroy operations against large enemy formations in Dinh Tuong and Long An provinces. Six major operations were conducted.

The MRF first went into action in the Rung Sat, in a search-and-destroy mission code named Silver Raider I. In mid-May 1967 it teamed up with Game Warden forces to carry out the largest riverine operation in the Rung Sat. Shortly afterwards, an even larger operation, Hoptac XVIII, saw the MRF in IV Corps between the Rach Ba Bau and Rach Tra Tan rivers, where very heavy fighting ensued. The encircled VC units lost over 100 men, while the MRF suffered few casualties and little damage to the boats.

One of its largest sweep-and-search operations took place on 11 June 1967 when heavily laden boats left

Strike force

TROOP INSERTION: With a rifle-toting officer in the lead, a platoon from the 9th Division, part of the Mobile Riverine Force, splashes through the mud to the bank of the My Tho River after being inserted by an ATC in September 1967. By this stage in the war draftees' combat gear had become more personalized. The soldier at right has a camera and a bottle of insect repellent tucked into his helmet strap. Graffiti on his helmet reads ''Chicago's best.'' His buddy has ''The New Yorker'' written on his.

their anchorages on the My Tho River near Dong Tam to steam 60 miles in the oppressive summer monsoon heat to Nha Be, which they reached the following day.

For the next four days infantry from the 9th Division, which had been embarked on the ATCs, conducted a wide-ranging sweep of the Rung Sat, supported by the Monitors of River Assault Flotilla One.

Running down the river to the South China Sea and then upriver to Nha Be had been uneventful, even agreeable. But the four days in the Rung Sat during Operation Great Bend were an ordeal. The place was a huge mangrove swamp, with few areas of dry land. The only signs of life were a few villages, impoverished even by Vietnamese standards, and some charcoal-making kilns. This was Viet Cong territory and every bend of each waterway held the promise of a machine gun burst or a rifle grenade.

On 18 June the river force moved its anchorage eight miles to reduce the travelling time to the Can Giouc district, where it was to launch operations the next day. The 3rd and 4th battalions of the 47th Infantry were embarked and, escorted by Monitors and helicopter gunships, headed for the landing sites. Five rifle companies landed in the north and swept south towards blocking positions established the previous night by a battalion of the 25th ARVN Infantry Division.

The sixth rifle unit, Company C of the 4th Battalion, landed in the south, where it moved to an assembly area as the force reserve, ready for commitment by boat or helicopter.

Late that morning a VC battalion was located east of the ARVN positions. The reserve company was sent in by helicopter to reconnoiter the enemy, but no contact was made. But Company A of the 4th Battalion, which was advancing in the west across open ground, suddenly came under heavy fire and took heavy casualties. The enemy were not where they were first reported. The other rifle companies soon moved against the enemy, who were well dug-in, their bunkers impervious to all but the heaviest projectiles. It took all the combined fire of the Monitors, helicopters, and barge-mounted artillery to penetrate the enemy positions. However at nightfall the fighting ceased.

The advance was resumed at daylight, but only

Bunker breaker —Zuni rockets are hurriedly loaded into the rocket pod of a UH-1B Iroquois helicopter of Light Helicopter Attack Squadron Three (HAL-3) on the flight deck of the converted tank landing ship *Jennings County*. On target the 2.75-inch Zuni was effective against canal bank bunkers.

one VC platoon was encountered—the rest had slipped away during the night. The remaining VC were quickly surrounded and wiped out. The bare facts contained in such post-action reports do little to convey the feel of a 60-foot armored troop carrier, exposed to the tropical sun, enveloped in diesel fumes, and packed with sweating troops moving up a narrow waterway that offers little visibility and encourages enemy ambushes. Equally difficult to convey is the strange suspension of time as the soldier lands and begins his slow advance on foot in hostile territory, or as the sailor maneuvers his slow boat under enemy fire or exposes himself to man his

Strike force

ACTION STATIONS: A PBR crew and Vietnamese Marines stand to their guns as a PBR captain puts on full throttle. PBRs carried very heavy firepower for such small boats. They were armed with three .50-caliber machine guns, and on some boats an M-60 machine gun and a 40mm grenade launcher—as well as an assortment of ad hoc weaponry, including 90mm recoilless rifles, 60mm mortars, flamethrowers, and 20mm cannon. The round object on top of the cabin is the radar scanner.

weapon in a firefight that invariably occurs at murderously close range. Only the bare statistical facts—46 US Army, 15 US Navy casualties and 225 Viet Cong—begins to record the enormity of what was, by both sides' standards, a minor operation.

From the sailors' point of view it was difficult to imagine how the VC could survive the full impact of US guns—let alone be in a position to shoot back. "The ships were very impressive when they returned fire, those 40mms could put out an awful lot of firepower," recalled one riverine veteran. "I guess the enemy really didn't have anything to match that in rate of fire and when you have five, six ships

On target —A Black Pony OV-10 Bronco fires a Zuni rocket at a ground target during a mission over the Delta. Originally intended as a reconnaissance plane, the all-weather Bronco served as an effective ground attack plane capable of hitting enemy targets too hazardous for helicopter attacks.

firing on the bank it's hard to imagine that anybody could stay out there and continue to fire."

Nearly a month after this operation, on July 25, the MRF, then based in Long An, received intelligence of an enemy build up in Dinh Tuong. It was ordered to shift to an anchorage near the Dong Tam base, eight kilometers west of My Tho.

Within 48 hours, the MRF had assembled its 4,000 men and boats, shifted its afloat base 100 kilometers and prepared to engage in the largest MRF operation of the war.

By 27 July, the 7th ARVN Division had started a sweep to the west, moving north of Highway 4 in the direction of Enemy Base Camp 470. Next day, the MRF moved into the Cam Son area and Vietnamese Marines deployed into the Ban Long area the day after.

During this operation the 9th Division had under control of its 2nd Brigade both the 5th Battalion, 60th Infantry (Mechanized) and the 3rd Battalion, 39th Infantry on call at its Long An base camp. The 9th also had operational control of a brigade of the 25th US Division based at Dong Tam. Meanwhile, Task Force 116, the Game Warden force, was maintaining a 30-boat patrol on the My Tho River between Sa Dec and My Tho.

On the night of the 28th, the 5th Battalion started a sweep towards the southwest, while the 3rd and 4th battalions of the 47th Infantry went north by river. Late in the morning the 3rd Battalion came under harassing fire. Shortly before dark an ATC took a direct rocket hit, which caused 25 casualties. Then the enemy disappeared.

The 7th ARVN Division had not encountered any VC forces, leading commanders to believe that the enemy was concentrated in the Ban Long area. The 3rd Vietnamese Marine Battalion Corps was landed there next morning. The landing was uneventful, but the battalion soon encountered strong enemy forces. The brigade of the 25th Division was deployed to the east to block off possible escape lines. By late afternoon, with the firefight still continuing strongly, the 3rd Battalion, 47th Infantry was ordered into a blocking position west of the combat area; the 4th Battalion was withdrawn to Dong Tam for a brief rest. The Vietnamese Marines launched a night attack that proved inconclusive; the enemy

counterattacked, causing heavy casualties on both sides but without breaking out. Late the next morning the 5th Battalion was moved into a new blocking position, while the 3d and 4th Battalions closed the cordon, surrounding the enemy. The enemy losses totalled 300, mostly from the Viet Cong 263rd Main Force Battalion; the Vietnamese Marines, which bore the brunt of the fighting, suffered 149 casualties; the MRF lost 38 men killed and wounded.

This four-day operation, which relieved a major threat to My Tho and Dong Tam, demonstrated the large numbers of troops required for an effective search-and-destroy mission. But even when the numbers were available for such operations, an elusive foe that knew the terrain could usually find a way to escape the encircling movements of the MRF. One river veteran put it like this: "Once you

FLOATING BATTERY: Seven-by-five floating pontoons linked together to form an artillery barge, manned by members of B Battery, 3rd Battalion, 34th Artillery in the 9th Infantry Division, being pushed into position on the riverbank to support an infantry operation.

Strike force

POINT BLANK: A 105mm howitzer provides close fire support for an operation near the Saigon River. Waterborne artillery support was a vital component in the MRF's flexible response, either carried on a pontoon raft or in the early days, as in this 1967 picture, in a converted landing craft (LCM).

turn off the main rivers, the VC in general know where you are going and have several hours to neutralize you." As soon as the MRF left their bases, spying eyes along the riverbanks constantly relayed information about the MRF's movements to the VC.

In September, another landing and sweep of the eastern Rung Sat uncovered a Viet Cong arsenal: 105 rifles and machine guns; 165 grenades; 60 howitzer and mortar shells; 56,000 rounds of small-arms ammunition; a small hospital; and 850 pounds of medicine. By the standards of the US logistic effort into South Vietnam's ports and airfields this

was small fry—but the VC had put their backs into carrying these supplies across mountain trails, and risked life and limb transporting them along rivers in the curfew. It would take them weeks to replace, and in the meantime their fighting effectiveness was severely impaired and their ability to treat wounded men much reduced—a further blow to morale.

But the Mobile Riverine Force did not have the fighting all its own way. The VC had teeth and often drew blood. The ambusher always held the advantage and a well-trained infantryman equipped with armor-piercing weapons could make life very

Flying teeth —The Seawolf insignia of HAL-3, the Navy's Helicopter Attack (Light) Squadron Three, a vital ingredient of the river war.

dangerous for a boat crew. During Operation Coronado V, in September 1967, the VC set up an ambush on a two-mile section of the Ba Rai River southwest of Saigon. After four hours, half the convoy had been hit by enemy fire, three Black Berets had been killed, and 77 had been wounded.

In October and November the MRF reported troop concentrations north of the Mekong Delta between Sa Dec and Dong Tam. The enemy proved elusive, but next month the VC struck back, ambushing River Assault Division 112 on the Ruong Canal northeast of Sa Dec.

However, the heavily armed sailors and soldiers fought through the ambush and turned the enemy's flank. Joining up with other US and Vietnamese forces, they surrounded the VC, killing 266 and seizing 5,000 rounds of ammunition, and over 300 small arms.

In June 1968 the 3rd Brigade of the 9th Infantry Division arrived to serve with the MRF. At the same time a third River Assault Squadron, 13, was formed. And a fourth, 15, was promised, along with additional barracks and repair ships.

By July the MRF was divided into Mobile Riverine Groups Alpha—containing squadrons 9 and 11—and Bravo—made up of squadrons 13 and 15. At the same time the 9th Division's battalions were given lighter equipment loads to enhance their air mobility. That month the 2nd Brigade was assigned to Kien Hoa province and also charged with pacification objectives.

This shift in strategy from strike operations to pacification was accompanied by a move of the 9th Division headquarters to Dong Tam.

Soon its air resources were reallocated to land brigades, forcing the 2nd Brigade to rely on Navy ATCs for mobility. All these factors served to reduce the MRF's capabilities and effectiveness when the Viet Cong had learned to fear the Americans' deadly riverine forces and to do everything they could to avoid meeting them in combat.

The VC now concentrated on deploying small "hunter-killer" teams in ambushes along the major waterways, causing higher casualties among US and Vietnamese forces. Enemy losses were now calculated at 1:5 for every friendly casualty, compared with 2:6 when the MRF was operating under more aggressive orders. Sometimes, however the ambushers themselves fell prey to a well-led opponent, as on 15 September 1968, when Assault Division 111 was ambushed on the Ben Tre River in Kien Hoa province. Although the division's commander, Lieutenant Charles J. Cox, received painful shrapnel wounds early in the engagement, he was able to evaluate the tactical situation with care and chose perfect landing sites for his infantry. The enemy quickly found themselves attacked from both flanks and suffered heavy losses, while the US infantry sustained few casualties. The skirmish, which won Lieutenant Cox the Navy Cross, was a textbook example of the flexibility and recovery power of riverine forces.

The Army's riverine force regained its helicopter support in October, restoring the MRF's effectiveness in time for wide-ranging operations—chiefly the next major phase of the riverine campaign, Sea Lords, which was about to begin. In November, Mobile Riverine Group Alpha was reassigned to support the 9th Division in the eastern Delta with five river assault divisions—91, 92, 111, 112, and 151. Bravo, with three divisions—121, 132 and 152—was dispatched to the western Delta.

EAST MEETS WEST: A Vietnamese family in a sampan paddles past an awesome mass of US Navy Monitors lined up on a canal bank in the Mekong Delta. Mom and dad look a little nervous, but the children have seen it all before: All their memories are of war.

Saviors of the Delta

THE VIET CONG'S surprise Tet Offensive, launched on 30 January 1968, provided the Mobile Riverine Force with its greatest challenge. It is one the MRF met completely. With its combination of firepower and mobility it first fought the enemy to a standstill, then rolled him back and hunted him down. General Westmoreland, the commander of US forces in Vietnam, was succinct in his praise: "The MRF saved the Delta." This success on the floating field of battle earned the MRF the Presidential Unit Citation.

Both sides paid a high price for Tet. The Viet Cong and the North Vietnamese Army (NVA) suffered some 58,000 casualties—many of them their most experienced soldiers. The American and South Vietnamese forces lost nearly 10,000 men. Harder to calculate but just as great was irreparable damage to the credibility of the US effort in Vietnam. Until the Tet Offensive, a determined assault on a multitude of key military and urban installations, this was a war the US public thought that America was winning. The Tet Offensive bought with it prime-time TV pictures of a bomb-devastated Saigon, of civilians fleeing from a bomb-damaged US Embassy in Saigon, the Great Seal of the United States lying in a heap of rubble by an embassy wall. A minor incident in the context of Tet, the direct attack on the embassy was a major shock for the US public.

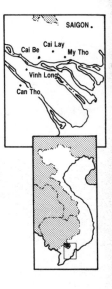

The offensive began on 30 January, when the lunar New Year celebrations were at their height, with attacks on eight towns and cities in the central highlands and central coastal plain. The main attacks followed the next day. More than 70,000 VC and regular North Vietnamese Army troops were committed to the assault; 36 of the 44 provincial

Bronco riders —The insignia of the Black Ponies of the Light Attack Squadron (VAL-4). Adapted from the aircraft they flew, the OV-10 Bronco, it was both a nickname and call sign.

capitals of South Vietnam were attacked, as were 64 of 242 district capitals and five of the six autonomous cities. These attacks were not hit-and-run terrorist operations like the VC's previous efforts, but determined attempts to fight their way into urban areas and hold them. (Once the Communists were there, all their perceived or potential enemies were slaughtered, with extreme cruelty.) Among the enemy objectives in the Mekong Delta were My Tho, Vinh Long, Can Tho, Ben Thie, Cai Lay, and Cai Be, but they were frustrated by the combined efforts of the Mobile Riverine Force and the 9th Infantry Division. During Tet the MRF was to be in action continuously for 30 days. The only breaks were to allow the men to snatch some sleep and give the boats some maintenance. In the first three months of the year the Mobile Riverine Base was to steam about 1,000 kilometers while conducting operations in Dinh Tuong, Vinh Long, and Phong Ding provinces.

When the Communists struck, the MRF had been dispersed along the major waterways in four fire support bases in Dinh Tuong and Kien Phong provinces to deny the VC communication lines across the Delta. The infantry were kept busy protecting the bases and patrolling adjacent areas.

The first job was to reassemble the scattered units into a strike force. Then two battalions were landed in My Tho, which had been overrun by the Viet Cong. It took three days of fierce street fighting to clear them out.

The next objective was to cut off the retreating VC at Cai Lay, but the enemy escaped, with little contact being made.

Then the MRF moved on to Vinh Long, to help the battered ARVN troops. The MRF moved into the south of the city, cutting the enemy's line of retreat with boats and ground forces. By 6 February the threat to Vinh Long had been broken, as had three battalions of the enemy. On 8 February the MRF was directed towards Saigon, where it remained until the enemy offensive there collapsed. For the rest of February fierce fighting continued around Can Tho, in the Delta.

There next followed a succession of small-scale actions. The enemy had learned the high price of tangling with the greater firepower and mobility of the

MRF and was reluctant to take the large losses resulting from bringing large numbers of troops into action. Instead the Viet Cong reverted to their most effective and tested tactic, the ambush.

IN THE DELTA, just as elsewhere in Vietnam, Tet had acted as a watershed. The Americans had lost their air of invulnerability. For the Viet Cong the Tet Offensive was an expensive failure, but one that had shown that American forces could be challenged and driven off—however temporarily.

One river boat captain noted the changes: "After Tet this whole country really changed. Anybody that has been here before and has come back again can't deny that it has changed.

"All hell broke loose in Tet. The place I was at, called Vinh Long, the VC really tore the place up and I think the Americans more or less got blamed for it. We had to evacuate the town and when we did go back into Vinh Long I think there was quite a few Vietnamese people around who kind of looked

LOOKING FOR TROUBLE:
Two Broncos from Light Attack Squadron Four (VAL-4) fly low over the Rung Sat in search of the enemy. Ruggedly built and designed for counter-insurgency work, the Broncos are armed with pods of 5-inch Zuni rockets. The squadron insignia was a Black Pony.

A fiberglass-hull PBR, weighing scarcely 7 tons, is hoisted out of the water for repairs at the self-propelled mobile repair base at Tan My. The PBR's radar dome has been retracted to prevent it from fouling the top of the dry dock.

down on us a little for leaving them, you know, like we did. Things were pretty bad around Vinh Long for the next three or four months."

With the immediate crisis of Tet over, General Westmoreland called for a naval command under his operational control in the northern I Corps to coordinate security operations on the waterways, and keep supply lines open. I Corps Tactical Zone (ICTZ), which consisted of South Vietnam's five northern provinces and bordered the DMZ, was one of the most closely contested regions in South Vietnam.

On 24 February 1968, Task Force Clearwater was established in ICTZ under the command of Captain G.W. Smith.

Clearwater was to have responsibility for the rivers, canals, lakes, and estuaries from Da Nang to the DMZ in the north.

Its duties were to run convoys and provide escorts—to keep vital supplies flowing to the American and South Vietnamese forces. In 1967 about 90 percent of the supplies required for the friendly forces in those provinces came by coastal shipping and river boats.

At the end of 1967 the North Vietnamese were reckoned to have 15,000 regular troops in ICTZ's two northernmost provinces, Quang Tri and Thua Thien. Task Force Clearwater comprised two task groups based on the ports of Hue on the Perfume River and Dong Ha on the Cua Viet River. The two rivers were essential to maintaining effective control over Quang Tri and Thua Thien provinces.

The Hue group was made up of River Division 55, with ten PBRs and four converted LCM(6) minesweepers. Based at Dong Ha was River Assault Division 112, with one CCB, three Monitors, five LCM minesweepers, and ten ATCs. Cua Viet was an inhospitable place with no means of providing safe maintenance areas. The frequent artillery attacks from the Demilitarized Zone made construction work a dangerous proposition. Instead, it was decided to transport PBRs needing maintenance from Cua Viet to the mobile base MB1, 40 miles southeast at Tan My, by means of a self-propelled dry dock. This was an LCM-8 fitted with skids to support a PBR on the well deck and equipment to pump water in and out of the side walls, so that the craft could lower itself in the water and allow a PBR to sail right on

Saviors of the Delta

THE SMALLEST AIRCRAFT CARRIER IN THE WORLD: A medevac helicopter evacuates a wounded man from an ATC converted into a hospital boat ATC (H), during Operation Coronado V. **BELOW:** Deckside view as a wounded man is lifted from a Monitor onto a helicopter waiting aboard an ATC(H). Nicknamed the micro flat-tops, the converted armored troop carrier hospital boats were assigned to the various river assault flotillas stationed in the waterways of the Mekong Delta.

111

board. This ingenious device could be used even
during the violent northeast monsoon.

The enemy mounted large ambushes, extracting
a heavy toll on the Clearwater boats, and it soon
became clear that speed rather than armor increased
the chances of survival against ambushes from
rockets and grenades. (In fact the ASPBs, the steel
assault support patrol boats, were in some ways
more vulnerable. Whereas an RPG would often go
straight through the fiberglass hull of a PBR
because there was no resistance to detonate the
warhead, the steel ASPBs provided the frame for the

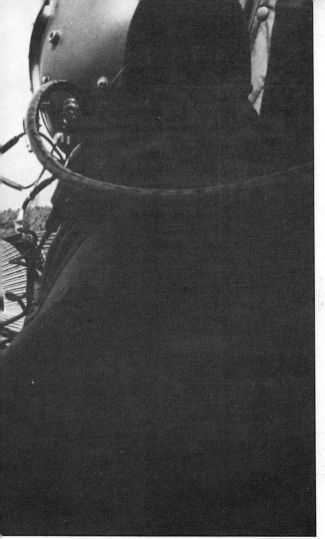

Saviors of the Delta

AVENGER IN THE SKY: The right door gunner of a Sea Wolf gunship prepares for a firing run over a VC ambush site located on a riverbank of the Mekong Delta. The helicopter was answering a distress call from the blazing PBR below. Minutes earlier it had been hit by recoilless rifle fire.

RPG to explode on—showering its crew with potentially lethal shrapnel.) Accordingly, a request was made to replace the armored river assault boats with more of the faster, more maneuverable PBRs. A second section of ten boats from the Rung Sat arrived in Cua Viet by June, making possible the withdrawal of River Assault Division 112. Three of the air cushion PACVs, which had been operating in the Mekong Delta, were sent to augment forces around Hue, while eight LCPLs adapted for night surveillance were sent up to Dong Ha.

The enemy continued to be active on other fronts.

A second wave of post-Tet attacks was launched throughout March, April, and May—again at heavy cost to the aggressors. In the fighting to relieve pressure on Saigon, the MRF destroyed a large formation of VC south of the capital and badly mauled the 514th Main Force Battalion near Cai Lay. In addition the MRF estimated they inflicted nearly 700 casualties on other enemy forces besieging the capital.

In the north the battle for the city of Hue had been won by June 1968 and the Perfume River that surrounded the ancient citadel had been pacified. The American sailors were back on top and could return to the offensive. So the Clearwater's mission was expanded. In addition to its successful convoy and escort duties, the boats were now to "conduct riverine operations on the Perfume and Cua Viet rivers and adjacent waterways."

In effect the Clearwater forces could now engage in ambushes, search-and-destroy missions, psychological operations, and regaining active control of the immediate territory and its people for the Saigon government.

The many lagoons that provided hiding places and strike bases for the enemy were prime targets and, working in harness with the 101st Airborne

Division, Task Force Clearwater cleared out the Viet Cong from Vinh Loc Island.

On the Cua Viet the NVA stepped up their mine attacks in response to this initiative, putting the 3rd Marine Division security units on the river banks under great pressure to increase their vigilance.

However, the deployment of three MSBs early in 1969 from Mine Division 113 soon ended Charlie's underwater efforts. In the Delta the emphasis also moved to offensive operations. Come July and August 1969 the MRF was able to roam at will through the Mekong Delta at full strength. In the last tactical operation with Vietnamese and US ground troops, the allied forces smashed into the VC stronghold of the U Minh forest, in the west of the Delta. The VC fought back viciously and at great cost to the allied expedition. But the armored force prevailed, stayed put, and denied that sanctuary to the enemy.

The Viet Cong military strategy continued to follow the classic guerrilla pattern: Retreat when the enemy attacks; harass when he stands; and attack when he retreats. As the enemy backed off from large-scale confrontation, the American Army bowed out of riverine operations, handing over its reduced role to the South Vietnamese Army, while the MRF moved over to pacification work and trained Vietnamese personnel to operate its craft. The transfer of the US Navy's assets under the Vietnamization program began on 1 January 1969.

This transfer took place against a backdrop of constant harassment by the Viet Cong. In June 1969, there were 19 attacks against shipping in the Long Tau approach to Saigon. But no Vietnamese Marines or MRF forces were available to clear out the "backyard." So a task force of Australian and Thai units was set up on 22 June to clear out a large VC sapper unit lurking in the Rung Sat. These allied forces gave the VC short shrift and the following month only two attacks were made against shipping.

Australian, Thai, Vietnamese, and American forces kept up attacks on enemy bases in the Rung Sat, maintaining a continuous ground presence in an area that had been jealously regarded by the VC as a safe transit zone. The lesson had been learned late.

Meanwhile pacification was proving a difficult

Safe behind bars —The helmsman of an ATC keeps an eye on the river from his wheelhouse. The bar armor gave protection while permitting ventilation and visibility for the lowest possible weight penalty. The bars could detonate the warhead of a rocket-propelled grenade without producing the jet of molten metal these weapons normally created when they hit steel plate.

process. Given the opportunity, Charlie always slunk back to a newly cleaned sanctuary if allowed.

But as soon as he was driven off for any length of time pacification programs could take root. Abandoned settlements in the Rung Sat were reoccupied and their dormant economies quickly revived.

Tet was assessed as a failure for the Communists; they had failed to take and hold any major population centers; there had been no popular uprising of the people; no shattering of the capability or will of

the ARVN, nor destruction of US military power.

For the American forces the Tet Offensive proved a pyhrric victory. It had cost them US public opinion. When General Westmoreland requested more men to help him ram home that victory, President Johnson not only refused but also ordered troop levels frozen.

It was a turning point.

A military disaster for the North Vietnamese had been turned into a political one for the South.

HOME AND DRY:
Troops of the 3rd Battalion, 47th Infantry Division, return from a mission to their floating base for hot showers and air-conditioned comfort.

On the barrier

AS 1968 CAME to its end, and ironically as the mood in Washington began to turn against the war, the Navy high command felt ready to embark on a more aggressive strategy, one destined to take its riverine task forces into the farthest reaches of the Delta, as far inland as Tay Ninh, nearly 100 miles from the sea.

Here the rivers run more swiftly, clumps of tree limbs and brush sweep by in the current, making swimming dangerous—but reducing the danger from saboteurs. Before the defoliants did their work, the banks were dark and overgrown compared to the desolate stretches of mud further down in the Delta. Most patrols were carried out at night, a night often bright with the white glow of illumination rounds fired for hours at a stretch over the nearby Cambodian border.

Sea Lords (Southeast Asia Lake, Ocean, River, and Delta Strategy), as the new concept was called, was an umbrella for several different operations that shared the same objective: using the Navy's riverine forces to establish control over the land area of the Mekong Delta. Its first priorities were three: to cut Viet Cong infiltration and supply routes into the Delta; to establish permanent control over the main cross-Delta waterways; and to penetrate the enemy-held Ca Mau peninsula, the last great VC stronghold in the area.

It was a highly ambitious program. For the first time in the Vietnam War it was proposed to establish a line that the enemy could not cross, that most elusive thing in a guerrilla war: a front line. Behind that barrier the enemy could be harried to destruction with a greater chance of success, his

HOT WORK: A Swift boat crew in action, during a raid on the Ca Mau, firing a pedestal-mounted .50-cal machine gun, a hand-held M-79 grenade launcher, and a light machine gun.

territory divided up and finally penetrated and neutralized.

The Sea Lords strategy drew its roots from a variety of sources. As early as 1964 it had been recognized that the coastal blockade would be to some extent futile as long as it was solely an offshore operation. It had to be imposed, and it cost the enemy men and resources. But he was quite easily able to reroute supplies, particularly in the south, where large quantities of material from the Soviet Union were being landed at Sihanoukville, (now Kampong Som) in Cambodia and then moved inland on the so-called Sihanouk Trail into the Delta.

But in 1964 the Navy did not have resources to create a barrier in the Delta. By 1968 the political situation had changed and the Navy had accumulated enough resources to begin to push events the way it wanted, rather than simply trying to react and defend against enemy initiatives.

The success of the coastal blockade meant that the Swift PCF boats could be spared from endless hours patrolling in the Gulf of Thailand and the South China Sea. The Swift's combination of speed and hitting power was very much part of the Sea Lords concept, which the Navy had been considering for more than four years. The Mobile Riverine Force

—Men from Harbor Clearance Unit One tension a block-and-tackle device being used to refloat a sunken vessel in the Cai Lo canal. Viet Cong sabotage attempts concentrated on sinking vessels in the major waterways that provided supply lines for the US war effort.

also had surplus boats and crews because of the continuing shortage of ground forces with which to carry out combined operations.

It was a frustrating situation to have firepower lying unused, and the Navy was driven to look at ways of using its own spare resources effectively to take the place of ground troops.

Tactically, too, there had been a major change of heart during the Tet Offensive, when the PBR crews had reached such a level of confidence—and competence—that their two-boat combat patrols increasingly expected to take on enemy ambushes without assistance. In Saigon this brought the realization that it was Charlie who was now running scared. The time was right to come off the defensive.

Sea Lords was a joining together of Market Time, Game Warden, and Mobile Riverine Force techniques, with units from all three forces on loan to the new Task Force 194. The barrier patrols were, in strategic terms, the Market Time blockade taken far inland to the weed-choked canals along the

Cambodian border and the twisting river systems north of Saigon. They were backed up with the combined river/land tactics developed by the Mobile Riverine Force.

Although the strategy was drawn from previous operations, the crews experienced marked changes in their respective roles. The Market Time Swift boats were drawn into the lower reaches of the rivers to take over Game Warden tasks. The Game Warden PBRs meanwhile pushed inland. They were accompanied by the heavy assault squadrons of the MRF, which were broken down into small units and assigned to the various forward bases on a mission that placed less emphasis on large-scale troop lifts and much more on waterborne firepower.

Vice Adm. Elmo R. Zumwalt —boards USS *Crockett* in Cam Ranh Bay in October 1968 for a tour of inspection. As commander of Naval Forces in Vietnam, he was the principal architect of the successful Sea Lords concept.

One experienced MRF officer admitted that he had found it hard to make the transition; but not so the enlisted men, particularly the new arrivals. "The major consideration was that the new boat crews were not so much experienced and so concerned with heavy troop lift. . . . I don't think they were prejudiced against interdiction as the old-timers were."

Operations on the Sea Lords barrier were unfamiliar and crews were more prone to stress. There were fewer of the easy times sunbathing on deck during transits down the big rivers, and more nights of tension waiting in ambush staring into the gloom so hard the eyes begin to play tricks, so that three or four members of a crew might swear they could see an enemy soldier close on the bank, despite the evidence in the weird green glow of the starlight scope. When a firefight started it was without warning and at terrifyingly close range, sometimes less than ten feet.

More enlisted men and officers had to be taken off the river with psychological problems caused by the unending stress. This caused little resentment: On the front line it was understood that every man had his breaking point; it was mostly a question of when he reached it.

Officially, also it was recognized that there was no scope for nursing a man back to combat fitness on a PBR with a crew of four. Overall the ease with which men were transferred out of the most intense combat zones probably contributed to the high morale that was consistently reported.

The logical place for the first Sea Lords barrier to

be established was along the Vinh Te canal, which closely parallels the Cambodian border from the Gulf of Thailand to the Bassac River. However, the Navy had taken political flak in past border incidents, and instead decided to set up the first rather tentative interdiction line on the Rach Gia-to-Long Xuyen canal. First the canal was penetrated by a mixed force of PBRs and assault craft, a mission that was accomplished in five days against light resistance, then a regular patrol was established. Operation Search Turn, started on 2 November 1968, had the virtue of taking the shortest line from

On the barrier

ENEMY TERRITORY: PCFs laden with Vietnamese troops sail up a narrow tributary to a landing zone in the Ca Mau peninsula during April 1969. The area was considered safe enough for the PCFs to travel in close formation. The US Navy provided the bulk of the sea power for operations in the Ca Mau, but the ground forces were Vietnamese Marines.

the Bassac to the gulf, but it was something of a dummy run and excluded a large chunk of the northwestern Delta.

The Vinh Te canal was meanwhile placed off limits.

However, the high command's caution was not always reflected at lower levels, and it so happened that reserve Lieutenant (j.g.) Michael Bernique, patrolling the Gulf of Thailand in his Market Time PCF, decided to put into Ha Tien, at the seaward end of the Vinh Te canal, for a break.

Sure enough he was told by villagers that Viet

125

Close support —A Navy Iroquois helicopter provides air cover for a PCF patrol on Operation Giant Slingshot. The bond between boat crew and airmen was reinforced by constantly working together, and it was a vital element in the success of riverine operations.

Cong "tax collectors" had set up shop a few miles up the Rach Giang Thanh, the waterway that leads into the canal.

Lieutenant Bernique wasted no time in moving his PCF's area of operations inland, and opened fire on the surprised tax station at less than 100 yards range, killing three of the seven Viet Cong, and capturing a quantity of arms and documents. The other VC fled, counterattacking a few minutes later, unsuccessfully, at a cost of two more dead and two wounded. At this point, having inflicted 100 percent casualties on the enemy force, the canny Lieutenant judged the moment right for a strategic withdrawal, back to the relative safety of the Gulf of Thailand.

His report on the action reached Saigon quickly once his superiors realized the implications of what he had done, and Lieutenant Bernique found himself outside the office of Vice Admiral Elmo R. Zumwalt Jr., ComNavForV, the chief of Naval forces in Vietnam, in a very short space of time. He would probably have preferred another meeting with some VC tax collectors. Bernique could have been court-martialled for disobeying standing orders, but he emerged from his interview with the Silver Star, and a new mission: Clear the Vinh Te canal! The Rach Giang Thanh was promptly renamed Bernique's Creek.

On 16 November 1968, Bernique led three Swift boats back into the canal, supported by Seawolf gunships in Operation Foul Deck. He again came under fire, and once more punished his attackers. The Navy's initial caution was justified when the Cambodian government at first protested that some of its civilians had been killed, but this was shown to be untrue by local investigations and film taken during the firefight. The operation continued, PBRs backed by assault craft pushed into the canal from the Bassac, the Swifts continued to move up from the Gulf of Thailand, and the Vinh Te was cleared, despite problems with the low water level in the canal.

Foul Deck was renamed Tran Hung Dao in its later stages, when the Vietnamese Navy took over a major share of the effort, and became the second most active of the Sea Lords interdiction barriers. Lieutenant Bernique's initiative, and his admiral's good sense, meant that the North Vietnamese were now facing severe communications problems in and out of the whole of the southern half of the Delta, down to the Ca Mau peninsula, an area of some 5,000 square miles. But that was not to be all.

Less than one month later the most ambitious of the four Sea Lords barriers was begun: Giant Slingshot. (It was named for the shape on the map drawn by the two rivers it was based on, the Vam Co Dong and the Vam Co Tay.) Its purpose was to cut off the notorious Parrot's Beak area of Cambodia, southern terminus of the Ho Chi Minh Trail.

Less than a month after that, on 2 January 1969, the line was completed when Operation Barrier Reef opened up the La Grange-Ong Lon canal between the Mekong River and the Parrot's Beak, thus joining the Giant Slingshot barrier to Operation Foul Deck.

The US Navy had established a continuous patrolled line running some 250 miles from the Gulf of Thailand to the mouth of the Saigon River. Coming so soon after the Tet debacle, it was a shattering blow to Hanoi.

Veterans had mixed emotions about operating the interdiction patrols. A crewman in an armored troop-carrier recalled the monotony: "We moved up

QUIET TIME: A PBR crew searches villagers' sampans close to the Cambodian border on Operation Giant Slingshot. The routine was boringly familiar, but crews had to keep an alert eye on the bank for ambushes. The patrol boat carries six men—four crew, the patrol officer, and an interpreter.

ZIPPO CRUISE:
A flamethrower-equipped Monitor of River Assault Flotilla One cruises along a narrow canal burning off the underbrush to deny the enemy any shelter for an ambush.

to Operation Giant Slingshot, about 15th March, and we stayed there until the 10th May. We were on the Vam Co Dong, the right arm of the Giant Slingshot, and our home base up there was Go Dau Ha. And we operated on routine patrols. We would steam maybe two hours north and steam maybe two hours back to the base, then the next night we would steam two hours to the south, and two hours back to the base.

"We were passing the PBRs. They were along the river bank set up in night ambush. They just sit there, very very quiet, then as soon as somebody'll

start moving across the river they'll crack the mike on the radio and whisper into the mike, so the modulation isn't too loud, and they would whisper there's somebody coming out now and get ready to fire, and they'll usually wait until two or three sampans are out in the middle of the river, then they'll kick on the engines and the minute they kick on those engines old Charlie knows he should have stayed home tonight, but he usually doesn't make it more than 5 or 6 feet anyway.

"They don't take prisoners because in a night ambush people go over the side or they get killed, and

Difficult landing —Vietnamese Marines clamber over the bow of a PCF into a bamboo thicket as it inserts them into a creek in the Ca Mau. Natural landing points were not always available in the marshlands of the Ca Mau.

most of them got killed, which is. . . the reason we're here. Very effective these night ambushes." Three patrols out of four took place at night, the favored time for movement by an enemy lacking control of the air.

Maintaining a force of small boats strung out over hundreds of miles of water created logistics problems. A divisional staff officer described the frustration of being unable to repair a boat. "The repair tender was down in the Vam Co river, the large tributary, and the people would be far advanced to support bases such as Moc Hoa and Ben Kyo and Tay Ninh, and Go Dau Ha. It took approximately 14 hours to go from Moc Hoa, for example, steady steaming to the tender and by the time you got the boat back you had got another problem as a result of the long transit. They particularly related to underwater fittings, screws, rudders. It was almost a rare occasion when you did have a boat with two screws.

"The engines, of course, being as old as they are, had all they could do to move that heavy boat so we were always encountering engine problems and electrical problems. The advanced tactical support bases were geared solely for PBR support. In the heavy assault boats we had to literally rely on our own assets to do any repairs, and a great deal of cannibalization went on. To keep two boats operating we had to cannibalize from a third. I guess nobody really enjoyed Giant Slingshot, in the squadron, simply because of the lack of availability of parts and certainly the tender. This proved to be the Achilles Heel.

"The boats simply did not operate for extended periods of time away from a support activity. They just can't."

The interdiction patrols were most effective, it was found, when ground troops carrying on vigorous day and night bank patrols worked together with the patrol boats constantly sweeping the waterways.

The Viet Cong needed reliable intelligence on the river patrols in order to mount successful crossing operations. This was difficult to obtain when the banks were constantly being patrolled by the Army. Where the waterborne patrols were as frequent as they were in Giant Slingshot, the only remotely safe way of moving men or supplies across a water

GROUNDED:
PCFs embedded in the side of a narrow channel after Vietnamese Marines have disembarked. The PCF's V-shaped bow made it easy to pull off the muddy banks.

obstacle was to hold the crossing unit hidden in readiness on the bank or in a side creek, hoping to rush across during a lull in patrols. When the bank itself was hostile terrain this became impossible.

To make the Sea Lords inland blockade strategy more effective, the command structure was decentralized. This allowed more initiative for junior ranks, and made it possible for units to respond faster to enemy moves. Attacks that would once have taken weeks to clear through a bureaucratic command structure could now be mounted within hours of receiving, say, a reliable intelligence report of an enemy supply run.

The organization was characterized by great flexibility and willingness to learn new tactics. Innovations included using giant Skycrane helicopters to airlift PBRs into apparently inaccessible waterways,

On the barrier

BIG LIFT: A US Army CH-54A Tarhe helicopter lifts a PBR out of Tan Chau, on the Mekong near the Cambodian border, for redeployment on the Cai Cai waterway further down into the Delta during Sea Lords. Many rivers and canals were impassable due to silting near their mouths, but perfectly navigable on long stretches further upstream. Helicopter lift opened up these Viet Cong safe areas.

which allowed the Navy to keep the Viet Cong continually off balance. At its most effective the Sea Lords barrier included electronic sensors, backed by the PBRs, in turn supported by infantry, Navy Sea Wolf helicopter gunships, and Black Pony Bronco close-support planes, plus artillery support from Army firebases.

There was a willingness to learn from the enemy, to understand his organization and tactics, even to turn his equipment against him, when captured

sampans were used to probe his canals. A prime illustration of this was the waterborne guard post, which adopted the Viet Cong's favorite technique, the ambush, and turned it back on him at the time he felt most secure: in the dead of night.

Routine patrols would continue while a guard post was set up at a point selected as a likely river crossing. The guard post commander would inform local ground forces of its location, so that artillery and mortar fire plans could be prepared, and then the two

PBRs would discreetly tie up in the darkness. The mooring lines would be passed loosely around trees so that they could be quickly cast off without a crewman leaving the boat. The bows were pointed straight into the bank, for several reasons. Broadside, the most likely target—a sampan crossing the river—could be engaged by all the weapons along the length of the boat at once, unlike a target ahead or astern; and, most important of all, the water jet was safely in midstream, so that a burst of the engine on full astern would pull them instantly clear of the bank with the least possible risk of getting stuck in the mud at the water's edge, or clogging the jet with debris.

A contemporary report by a naval staff officer cites "the high practitioner of the waterborne guard post in Vietnam" as Chief Signalman Bob Allen Monzingo. During his stint on the river as a patrol officer with River Division 593, Monzingo was awarded three Bronze and two Silver Stars. One of his more memorable engagements with the enemy occurred on the upper Saigon River in the summer of 1969. He set his two-boat guard post at dusk in the midst of a driving rainstorm, at a spot where the river runs shallow and relatively narrow. His men had just gotten into their ponchos and rain gear and were steeling themselves for a long, wet, and uncomfortable night, when word came from the cover boat as follows: "Chief, I see a bunch of them out there." Monzingo had to look several times to believe what he was seeing on the near bank, only a few dozen yards away in the gray gloom. Columns of enemy soldiers were filing past, heads lowered because of the driving rain, shoulders bent by the weight of heavy weapons, rocket launchers, and packs. He quickly estimated that there were at least 80 and perhaps a full company of the enemy. It seemed incredible that they were still unaware of the presence of the PBRs.

A whispered order into the radio mike and the engines in both boats leaped to life. They pulled back fast into the middle of the stream, simultaneously pouring fire into the surprised ranks of the enemy. The boats themselves were soon under fire from both banks and it was obvious that Monzingo's guard post had been set right in the middle of a planned large-scale crossing attempt by the Communist soldiers.

Helicopter gunships, tactical air, and artillery were called in to support the PBRs. The next morning 49 enemy dead were found.

Ambush and counterambush became part of the cat-and-mouse game of the Delta. Charlie learned to set traps for the ambush teams, setting up his own ambushers perhaps several nights before a supply run was due. When the PBRs discreetly eased themselves into the bank for their night's vigil, unfriendly eyes were watching. And when the Americans spotted a sampan slipping into midstream, suddenly they found themselves in a vicious fight, already virtually surrounded.

In one typical incident in Kien Giang province in the western Mekong Delta, the VC ambush was so close to the guard post chosen by a PBR team that Seaman Timothy D. Alspaugh was actually hit on the side by a grenade thrown from the underbrush the moment he spotted a boat moving on the river. He and the rest of the crew of his PBR had waited patiently for several hours in the shadow of a stand

Tug of war —A demolition team member ties a line to a wooden barricade built by the Viet Cong at the mouth of a river on the Ca Mau peninsula. Once secured, the line would be tied to a PCF and the obstacle pulled away.

of nipa palms, but the enemy had waited longer and more patiently than they. As Alspaugh brought his .50-cal machine gun to bear on the sampan he felt the grenade hit him. Then, in a moment that combined cool courage with sheer good luck, he spotted the grenade nestling in the bilge pump cover on the far side of his gun mount and still had time to throw it back into the trees as he opened fire. He was awarded the Navy Cross.

The Navy did not wait for the interdiction barriers to be completed before moving towards other Sea Lords campaign objectives: securing the Delta crossings, and penetrating and pacifying enemy strongholds. These were operations made possible, in part, by the slow strangulation of the interdiction

MESSY BUSINESS: Vietnamese Marines wade through thigh-deep mud at low tide on their return from a shore sweep near Old Cam Can in the lower regions of the Ca Mau.

lines, and in part by the crippling losses the Viet Cong had taken to achieve the political victory of Tet. In the course of 1969 Sea Lords units also moved to reinforce the Army in I Corps area in Operation Sea Tiger and into the Saigon River in Operation Ready Deck, which ran in parallel with the Giant Slingshot, a few miles further east.

But first attention was given, in November and December 1968, to clearing areas inside the Delta, including the banks and islands of the Bassac River, from the VC-held river crossing at Can Tho to the sea.

At the same time other forces began to press into the Ca Mau peninsula. As increasing numbers of PCF patrol boats entered the area, the Viet Cong reacted by building up defenses at the entrance to

Bunker blast —A member of a US Navy underwater demolition team prepares to blow up a Viet Cong bunker. The canal and riverbank bunkers provided the VC with their most effective attack points. They were impregnable to almost every sort of attack except heavy artillery. Destruction by gelignite was the only guarantee that the bunkers would not be used again.

the waterways. In response, just before Christmas, in Operation Silver Mace a riverine force made up of monitors, assault boats, and armored troop carriers, accompanied by an APB barracks ship and an ARL repair ship, moved out from Rach Gia, across the open sea, and smashed the defense works in a three-day assault.

The New Year brought a succession of operations in the Ca Mau, on a smaller scale, designed to stop the enemy restoring his position. Then in April came Silver Mace II, one of the last big troop lifts by the riverine force into the Ca Mau. The operation included 54 assault boats, 13 Market Time PCFs, Sea Wolves helicopter fire teams, and three battalions of Vietnamese Marines.

An officer in the Silver Mace II assault force remembers the sense of foreboding everyone experienced before going into the Ca Mau. It was Indian country—a remote region that had long been neglected by the Saigon government and exploited by the Viet Cong: "It was a very desolate and inhospitable area, very few signs of life. Not too many people lived in the area any longer, specially after the city of Nam Can (the region's capital) was destroyed. The few people that were there were predominately wood-cutters and very poor fishermen, and their existence was determined by the needs of the VC in the area. They were forced to cut wood, build bunkers and provide rice and man power. . ."

The VC response to the massive strike force of Silver Mace II was to go to ground and avoid all but minor contacts. Nonetheless the operation was considered to have considerably disrupted Viet Cong operations and to have begun to loosen its grip on the Ca Mau.

The breakthrough came two months later, thanks to a piece of naval engineering. A new kind of floating base first used in the Giant Slingshot interdiction operation, the Mobile Advance Tactical Support Base (MATSB), was located in the Cua Lon River near the ruins of old Nam Can city. It was constructed on nine pontoons and gave PCFs and river assault craft access to the sea either side of the peninsula, a strategic advantage in an area subject to strong monsoon winds that changed direction twice a year. The ATSB was also at the heart of

Operation Sea Float, as the pacification program in the region was called, which was a rapid success, not least because it involved considerable elements of the Vietnamese Navy.

Despite threats by the VC, thousands of visitors flocked to the Navy complex, drawn at first by curiosity in an area long controlled by the Viet Cong. Industry revived and within a few months more than 9,000 people had resettled in the vicinity of the base. Its success encouraged the setting up of a similar operation, on a slightly smaller scale, further north in the Ca Mau, in Operation Breezy Cove.

These major pacification efforts added to the success of Sea Lords by disrupting VC support inside the area cordoned off by the barrier patrol lines. Enemy forces inside the Delta were already feeling the pinch as supplies and communications with Hanoi were increasingly cut off. Faced with direct attack by the marauding Swift boats, and the Riverine Strike Group, which replaced the Mobile Riverine Force, they now found their economic base being undermined by the attractions of the safe prosperous areas

DAYBREAK:
The Mobile Riverine Force at their temporary base near old Nam Can. Nearest the camera is a Zippo Monitor, with its two bow-mounted flamethrower turrets, next to it a Monitor with an Amtrac-type 105mm gun turret, then a command-configured Assault Support Patrol Boat and an ordinary ASPB.

around the MATSB. While operations in the Ca Mau were continuing, a strong threat from NVA regular forces developed in July 1969 for the city of Tay Ninh, on the northernmost arm of Giant Slingshot.

It was rapidly countered by a massive concentration of 105 assault boats from both US and South Vietnamese units who had been deployed from all over the Delta. The operation had been made possible by the control achieved over the cross-delta waterways.

The US Navy could look upon Sea Lords as one if its successes. In its first year US forces had killed 3,000 Communist soldiers, captured some 300, and

On the barrier

WATER CONDO:
A Mobile Afloat Tactical Support Base (MATSB), constructed from ammunition pontoons, is towed up the Cua Lon River to its mooring off the city of old Nam Can. The base offered a variety of services to the civilian population, ranging from medical care to a sampan repair workshop. It quickly became the focus for a revival of the area's economy.

taken or destroyed 500 tons of weapons and supplies. By the end of the Sea Lords campaign all the original assignments had been successfully completed. And, at the same time, the US units involved had made their contribution to the ongoing process of Vietnamization, training their Vietnamese replacements so that they could take over the various riverine operations as going concerns.

After the US forces withdrew, things went less smoothly for the less experienced Vietnamese Navy, but they were able to keep the Delta secure right up until the fall of Saigon in 1975, so sound was the basic strategic conception introduced in Sea Lords.

The only way out

8

The ACTOV program

FROM 1968 ONWARD senior commanders had to devote increasing efforts to organizing the training of South Vietnamese forces to take over the Americans' combat roles.

The Vietnamization policy was formally adopted by newly elected President Richard M. Nixon early in 1969. It fitted in well with existing US Navy practice and thinking. With Navy forces in Vietnam being more than halved—down from a peak of 38,000 men in 1968 to 16,000 in 1970—an increasing amount of resources, especially advisors, had been devoted to training the Vietnamese.

The policy of handing over the conduct of the war to the Vietnamese, to be known as ACTOV (accelerated turnover to Vietnam) was vigorously put into effect by Vice Admiral Elmo Zumwalt, when he took over as Commander, Naval Forces, Vietnam in the fall of 1968.

His predecessor, Rear Admiral Kenneth L. Veth, had organized the handover of two river assault squadrons in mid-1968. Vice Admiral Zumwalt next set the goal of completing the transfer of the equipment and operational commands by the middle of 1970, followed by bases and logistical operations. However, the last of the Game Warden PBRs were not handed over until December 1970, and the transfer of the bigger Market Time ships took until the end of 1971.

It added up to a heavy training load, especially when both American and Vietnamese units were facing a series of major combat missions in the aftermath of Tet, and with Sea Lords just beginning.

One of the most difficult problems was how to avoid pulling thousands of men away from combat duties without, at the same time, reducing the

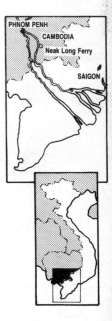

Armory advisor —A US naval advisor explains the operation of an 81mm mortar to a Vietnamese crewman. The Vietnamization program relied on American crews being replaced one-by-one by Vietnamese crew members.

pressure on the enemy. The Navy's solution was one-to-one training.

In this process individual Vietnamese were integrated into American units, at first as an extra man in a boat crew, or an extra officer in a headquarters. When they had mastered the skills, say of a PBR gunner, their American counterpart was withdrawn, and another Vietnamese brought in for training. When all the Americans had been replaced, command of the unit passed to the Vietnamese.

The first unit transferred under this system was River Assault Division 91 of the Mobile Riverine Force in January 1969. The Vietnamese Navy organized two River Assault and Interdiction Divisions (RAIDS) in its place, and these immediately joined the Sea Lords operations operating alongside US units.

By June another 64 river assault boats were handed over to the Vietnamese Navy, and River Assault Squadrons 9 and 11 were decommissioned. The 3rd Battalion of the 9th Infantry Division, which had been with the MRF from the start, was pulled out in July 1969. The following month, Task Force 117, the US Navy component of the Mobile Riverine Force, ceased to exist. It was the first major Navy command to be taken over by the Vietnamese. The new RAIDS plus the old River Assault Groups took over the MRF's role, which was somewhat lessened because of the effectiveness of Sea Lords, with Vietnamese Marines as the infantry element of the combined force.

By the end of April 1970 sufficient transfers had taken place to make the naval side of the invasion of Cambodia mainly a Vietnamese operation. ARVN ground forces crossed the border ten days before the Vietnamese Navy moved up the Mekong towards the Cambodian capital, Phnom Penh. The naval force, under Vietnamese command, included US PCFs, ASPBs, and PBRs, plus air detachments.

They were accompanied by base and logistics ships. The Vietnamese contingent included assault boats, PCRs, PBRs, and Marines.

Political restrictions on American involvement required US personnel to stop halfway to Phnom Penh at the Neak Long ferry. Eventually they were withdrawn by June 29, but the Vietnamese reached the capital and stayed, running convoys of supplies

and refugees up and down the river under increasingly heavy attacks from the Viet Cong and the Cambodian Khmer Rouge. The last supply convoy fought through to Phnom Penh with heavy losses in January 1975, just three months before the fall of Saigon.

The South Vietnamese Navy's performance at the outset of the invasion of Cambodia was significant in encouraging the transfer process.

By July 1970 the last of the Clearwater boats had been handed over to the Vietnamese Navy and by

JOINT OPERATION: A Vietnamese *Commandement*, a French-built command Monitor with American advisors on board during a US/Vietnamese operation.

December all the remaining PBRs and river assault craft were in Vietnamese hands. Game Warden became known as the Delta Naval Forces, with only Seals and naval aircraft as US backup until the final American withdrawal in 1973.

Control of the various Sea Lords operations passed to the Vietnamese as units completed their training. Operation Foul Deck, along the Cambodian border, became Tran Hung Dao I in March 1970.

The only way out

GOOD EXAMPLE:
A pipe-puffing bluejacket demonstrates the finer points of firing an M-60 light machine gun to an attentive audience of Vietnamese Marines. A C-ration can has been attached to the side of the weapon to alllow the ammunition belt to move smoothly through the breech.

Giant Slingshot became Tran Hung Dao II in May. The last Sea Lords operation to be transferred was Solid Anchor (originally Sea Float), the pacification program in the Ca Mau, in April 1971.

The handover of Market Time was phased. The PCFs and WPBs on the inner barrier operations nearest the coast were transferred by September 1970. Then, during 1971, the Vietnamese took on a number of ocean-going ships, including WHEC-class

Volunteer force —A militiaman from the Popular Civilian Forces (PCF) waiting to go into action from a PBR for a night ambush. These civilian irregulars were found to be most effective when operating in their home areas. When PCF units were deployed far away from their villages, they suffered unacceptable levels of desertion.

Coast Guard cutters armed with five-inch guns, and a radar picket ship. Finally, a coastal radar network was set up that was intended to take the place of US air surveillance. In 1971 approximately one North Vietnamese cargo trawler per month was detected by coastal forces, one ship getting through to the Ca Mau area and one being sunk, a performance that showed no deterioration from previous years.

When the last American ground forces left South Vietnam in March 1973, the Vietnamese Navy totalled 42,000 officers and men; 672 amphibious ships and craft; 20 minesweeping vessels; 450 patrol craft; 56 service craft, and 242 junks. It was the largest brown-water navy in the world.

There were mixed feelings over how effective it was going to be. The rapid expansion would clearly take some time to assimilate. And many of the problems of the Vietnamese Navy throughout the war remained: poor leadership, poor morale, lack of dedication among many personnel. The ARVN, Navy, Marines, and militia forces were capable of putting up a strong fight, according to one sailor who had fought alongside them. "On the PBRs I had ample opportunity to work with a lot of the Vietnamese, which was the Popular Forces in the Vinh Long area. And as far as I am concerned the majority of them had their act together. There was nothing in the world wrong with them people. They were just as brave as any Americans they got over here and they'll die just like any Americans." Not all felt the same way. Many US veterans were pessimistic at the time. One boat captain charged with the task of training a Vietnamese crew said: "I don't feel the Vietnamese are doing their share of the fighting to keep out the Communists. Dedicated fighters are few and far between. You can't make the Vietnamese keep proper watches." However, there was some deterioration in operational efficiency, mostly caused by maintenance problems. This was hardly surprising, given the lack of technical training and experience among the Vietnamese enlisted men and the wear-and-tear on equipment in riverine operations.

But the greatest contribution to the decline in the effectiveness of riverine operations was cuts in US aid, imposed by Congress. In 1974 budget constraints meant only 21 out of 44 riverine units could operate. In 1975 more than 600 river and harbor craft and 22 ships had to be mothballed to conserve resources.

However, the limited riverine force left to the South Vietnamese was never severely tested. The enemy did not target the waterways during 1973 and 1974. In 1975 coastal areas were to be the main operational area, but the collapse of the ARVN before the North Vietnamese advance was so rapid there was no scope for riverine intervention north of Saigon, and once Saigon had fallen the question of whether the Mekong Delta could be defended became academic. The conclusion of a Black Beret who had served two tours and had seen heavy action was to prove prophetic: "I just don't think they're going to make it by themselves. They're not quite ready yet."

NEW UNIT:
A solemn PBR gunner of the Vietnamese Navy's River Division 543 on the Cau Dai River for his boat's first patrol.
The pedestal mount in the stern carries a mortar and 7.62mm M-60 machine gun.

Last act of a tragedy

THE COMPLETION of the Sea Lords barrier in January 1969 was the result of one of the most remarkable naval campaigns in history.

A region that in 1966 was an enemy stronghold was turned around to the extent that it was the last significant area of South Vietnam to fall to the Communists.

A vast area of land had been captured and held by the world's greatest blue-water navy. The ocean-going might of nuclear submarines, battleships, and giant aircraft carriers had been abandoned for small boats in small channels, winning countless tiny skirmishes, waiting in ambush for pajama-clad platoons in the brown waters 100 miles from the sea.

It was a supreme example of the flexibility of sea power, made possible by the adaptability and open-mindedness of US Navy personnel at all levels, but above all by the bravery and fortitude of the men at the cutting edge of battle.

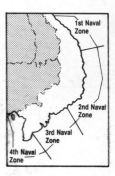

And that meant the most junior ranks, like the PBR crews, who took on heavy responsibilities and performed difficult and often delicate missions successfully. They did this while living in austere conditions, mostly in floating bases, under constant threat of ambush, carrying out operations mainly at night and suffering a steady hemorrhage of casualties.

Why was the riverine force so effective? One reason is the high morale reported at every level and shown by the numbers of medals awarded to the Black Berets, and by the rate at which men volunteered for second tours in Vietnam, despite the fact that at times one man in three could expect to get wounded or killed during his one-year tour.

Enlisted men and officers interviewed while the

war was in progress would speak of their units and their comrades with pride. They had a clear idea of what they were trying to achieve, and they could also tell that they were succeeding.

The very nature of the war for the boat crews was that it had to be fought in small teams. Loyalty to the team proved to be a very effective motivator in combat. Men who proved to be weak links could not be nursemaided in the front line, and the Navy took care to ship out quickly those who could not stand the strain.

Morale was also helped by the knowledge that the overall strategy was working and their resources were superior. The inland barrier patrols forced the Communists to respond, and gave the Navy boat crews the tactical advantage of defending their own turf. Better boats could carry heavier weapons and move them quickly to block attempts to break the

Last act of a tragedy

TEAMWORK:
Three Black Berets paddle a captured sampan back to their PBR "mother ship" after an unsuccessful search for a VC weapons cache. Nowhere else in the Navy were sailors given so much opportunity for individual initiative as in the small boats operating in Vietnam.

barrier. Advanced technology in the form of improved radar, the starlight scope for night vision, and the various electronic sensors used for surveillance were essential tools in running effective blockades.

Success in the Mekong Delta was also due to the Communists' failings. The Viet Cong never really mounted an efficient mining operation on the rivers, a failure only partly explained by the suggestion that they needed to use the waterways as well.

However they were brought about, the Navy's successes left the Saigon government in a controlling position in the Mekong Delta, the most vital single area for a viable South Vietnam, when President Richard Nixon launched his Vietnamization program.

The key to keeping the Communists out of the Delta was the Sea Lords barrier, which offered, for the only time in the Vietnam War, the real prospect

of long-term security. Behind that barrier the Viet
Cong were visibly losing the war; behind that barrier prosperity was visibly growing. These visible
trends were bound to have a powerful effect on
morale, both among the peasants and among the
men fighting to protect them.

The value of "psychological" operations and aid
schemes to give the people of the villages direct prac-
tical help, particularly with health care and building
projects, was quickly learned in the riverine war.

They had most dramatic effects in the deep south
of the Ca Mau peninsula, a remote backwater that
was one of the VC's biggest sources of support and
revenue in the Delta before Sea Lords.

Last act of a tragedy

FIGHTING SPIRIT:
A .50-cal gunner grits his teeth and aims low as he fires into VC positions on the banks of the Bo De River. Behind him a line of PCFs waits to take it in turns to make a firing pass at the enemy. This tactic of presenting a constantly moving target, while keeping up the flow of fire, was evolved during the riverine campaign.

But these psychological gains were frequently matched by psychological losses. Immediately on arrival on the rivers one US Naval officer saw members of the militia, the Regional and Popular Forces, routinely carrying out extortion on peasants in the Delta in exactly the same way as the VC tax collectors.

The Black Berets could do nothing about this: As disciplined fighting men their duty was to complete their mission without regard to the chaotic political situation. This they did with courage and efficiency second to none. The fact that their achievements were to be sacrificed at the negotiating table is part of the tragedy of Vietnam.

ARVN	— Army of the Republic of Vietnam (South Vietnam).
ASPB	— Assault Support Patrol Boat.
ATC	— Armored Troop Carrier.
BLT	— Battalion landing team.
CCB	— Command Communications Boat.
Charlie	— US troops' nickname for Viet Cong, based on Victor Charlie from the phonetic alphabet.
CINCPAC	— Commander in chief, Pacific.
CINCPACAF	— Commander in chief, Pacific Air Forces.
COMUSMACV	— Commander, US military assistance command, Vietnam.
CTZ	— Corps Tactical Zone, principal military and political territorial subdivision of the republic of South Vietnam.
Dinassaut	— French Naval Assault Division.
DMZ	— Demilitarized zone. Established by the 1954 Geneva accords, provisionally dividing Vietnam along the seventeenth parallel.
FAC	— Forward Air Controller. Pilot or observer who directs strike aircraft and artillery.
FOM	— French River Patrol Boat.
FSB	— Fire Support Base.
Howitzer, 105mm	— Standard light artillery piece with a maximum range of about 11,000m.
Huey	— Nickname for UH-1 series utility helicopters.
I Corps	— Military and political subdivision that included the five northern provinces of South Vietnam.
LCM	— Landing Craft, Mechanized
LCPL	— Landing Craft, Personnel, Large
LST	— Landing Ship, Tank
Lt (j.g.)	— Lieutenant (junior grade).
LZ	— Landing zone.
MACV	— Military Assistance Command, Vietnam. US command for all US military activities in Vietnam.

MATSB	— Mobile Advance Tactical Support Base.
MB1	— Mobile Support Base One.
MRF	— Mobile Riverine Force.
MSB	— Minesweeping Boat.
MSM	— Minesweeper (medium).
NVA	— North Vietnamese Army. Often used colloquially to designate a North Vietnamese soldier in the same way as ARVN was used to designate a South Vietnamese soldier.
PCF	— Fast Patrol Craft
PBR	— River Patrol Boat.
RAIDS	— River Assault and Interdiction Divisions.
RAG	— River Assault Group.
RPG	— Rocket-propelled grenade.
SEAL	— Sea Air Land Team—naval commando.
Sea Lords	— Southeast Asia Lake, Ocean, River, and Delta Strategy
Shaped Charge	— An explosive charge, the energy of which is focused in one direction.
Stab	— SEAL Team Assault Boat.
Swift boat	— Inshore patrol craft (PCF).
UH 1-B	— Single-turbine, single-rotor helicopter built by Bell.
VC	— Viet Cong.
Viet Minh	— Coalition founded by Ho Chi Minh in 1941. A contraction of "Viet Nam Doc Lap Nong Minh Hoi," the Communist-led coalition that fought the French.
Vietnamization	— Term given to President Nixon's phased withdrawal of US troops and transfer of their responsibilities to South Vietnam.
VNAF	— Vietnamese Air Force.
VNN	— Vietnamese Navy.
VNMC	— Vietnamese Marine Corps.
WPB	— Patrol craft adapted from 82-foot US Coast Guard cutter.

About the authors

John Forbes and Robert Williams

THE AUTHORS, John Forbes and Robert Williams, have edited several volumes in the *Illustrated History of the Vietnam War* series. When not writing or editing books together, they collaborate over war games.

John Forbes, a journalist and editor, has been a defense specialist for the *Western Daily Press*. He currently writes for a UK national newspaper.

Robert Williams is a senior editor for *The Times* in London. An honors graduate from Bristol University, where he studied US and Soviet affairs, he now intends to undertake a postgraduate course in strategic studies.

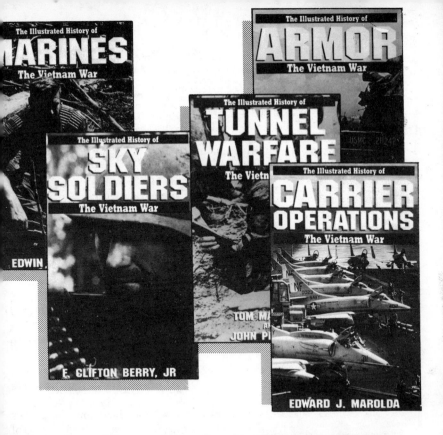

The Illustrated History of MARINES — The Vietnam War — EDWIN

The Illustrated History of ARMOR — The Vietnam War

The Illustrated History of SKY SOLDIERS — The Vietnam War — E. CLIFTON BERRY, JR

The Illustrated History of TUNNEL WARFARE — The Vietnam War — TOM MA... JOHN P...

The Illustrated History of CARRIER OPERATIONS — The Vietnam War — EDWARD J. MAROLDA

THE ILLUSTRATED
HISTORY OF
THE VIETNAM WAR

...m's Illustrated History of the
...am War is a unique and new
... of books exploring in depth the
...hat seared America to the core:
... that cost 58,022 American lives,
... saw great heroism and re-
...efulness mixed with terrible
...uction and tragedy.

... Illustrated History of the Viet-
...War examines exactly what hap-
...d: every significant aspect—the
...cal details, the operations and

the strategies behind them—is analyz-
ed in short, crisply written original
books by established historians and
journalists.

Some books are devoted to key battles and campaigns, others unfold the
stories of elite groups and fighting
units, while others focus on the role
of specific weapons and tactics.

Each volume is totally original and
is richly illustrated with photographs,
line drawings, and maps.